ACE ON THE RIVER

BARRY GREENSTEIN

ACE
ON
THE
RIVER

AN ADVANCED POKER GUIDE

FOREWORD BY DOYLE BRUNSON

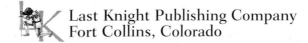
Last Knight Publishing Company
Fort Collins, Colorado

Last Knight Publishing Company
P.O Box 270006
Fort Collins, Colorado 80527

Ace on the River: An Advanced Poker Guide
A Last Knight Publishing Company Book / June 2005

10 digit ISBN: 0-9720442-2-1
13 digit ISBN: 978-0-9720442-2-6

Library of Congress Cataloging-in-Publication Number: 2001012345

All photography (with noted exceptions) by Gregg Kantz, New Renaissance Studio
Layout and design by Gregg Kantz, New Renaissance Studio

First Printing: June 2005

Printed by
Williamson Printing Company
Dallas, Texas 75235

Dateline: January 29, 2004. Tunica, Mississippi.

Announcer: *And it's an* **Ace on the River**, *giving Barry Greenstein Aces full. This is the first time two players have been knocked out on one hand at the final table in the history of the World Poker Tour.* *

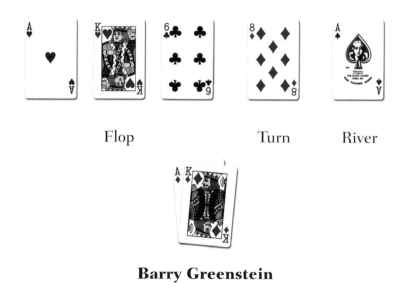

Flop   Turn   River

Barry Greenstein

*Actually, this had happened once before, but the announcer was not aware of it.

This book is dedicated to the children of gamblers. They were rarely promised anything, because the promise might have been too hard to keep. They may have wanted to play a game with their parent rather than watch a sporting event on which their parent had placed a bet. They were told everything was done so they could have toys and clothes and a nice place to live, but all they wanted was a little more of their parent's time. I apologize to my children, Michael Sebok, Joseph Sebok, Chris Sebok, Christina Tran, Nathaniel Greenstein, and Melissa Greenstein, for when I have failed as a parent.

TABLE OF CONTENTS

Foreword

by *Doyle Brunson*

Barry Greenstein is the consummate professional poker player. His attitude, demeanor at the table, and approach to the game sets him apart from most pros. The ability to maintain his composure in any situation is a trait I've long admired. His sense of fairness is unequaled to the point that he is almost always asked to arbitrate when there are disputes. I have watched Barry not only beat the biggest games, but destroy the best players in the world, consistently being the biggest winner, time after time.

Although Barry is in my top ten all-time best poker players, I respect him most for what he does outside the poker world. He has a giving nature and sets high standards for himself and the poker community. He is kind and gracious to everyone, almost to a fault. He is highly regarded for his honesty and integrity and is one of the most popular pros playing today.

Barry has received a lot of publicity for his philanthropy. He donates his poker tournament winnings to help underprivileged children. In the Jack Binion WPT in Tunica, Mississippi, he won the first place prize of over $1,200,000 and gave it all to help needy children. As a result, he is called The Robin Hood of Poker and has influenced many poker professionals, including me, to give to various charities.

I come from an era when poker players were regarded as second-class citizens, and I've seen poker evolve into the national pastime it is today. It has been a pleasure for me to watch Barry create goodwill for the greatest game on the planet.

I wrote *Super/System* in 1977 and *Super/System 2* in 2004 by collaborating with experts at each of the poker games commonly played at the time these books were written. I hope players will read my books to try to learn the games. I would then advise them to read *Ace on the River* to learn how to turn that knowledge into money.

Some interviewers have asked me what top players know that average players don't. I consider many of the differences to be matters of feel or instinct. These differences are difficult to put into words. However, Barry has put a framework on what the top players do and has written about some very high-level concepts. While I was reading his manuscript for the first time, I frequently said to myself, "Yeah, I know that, but I've never seen it described that way." This book contains a lot of stuff I knew but had never seen written — and some things I didn't know. *Ace on the River* is a book that no player will outgrow.

As the manuscript found its way into the hands of other top players, the question was asked, "What will the average player do with this knowledge?" This is the same question that was asked when *Super/System* first came out. Time has shown that players were able to absorb the complex concepts. I expect that will be the case here also. No beginner will become an expert as a result of reading any poker book, but after reading *Ace on the River*, many players will probably move to a higher level.

This book looks like candy to a poker player. As you skim through the examples, you feel, for the first time, that someone has shown poker hands the way they really are. Also, there are over a hundred photographs of places where I've played and people I've played with. It's my world on paper, in beautiful color. I enjoy just flipping through the book and looking at the pictures.

I understand very well what Barry went through in writing *Ace on the River*. As I did, he took time off during the prime of his career to write a book to educate players, some of whom are or will be his opponents. I often asked myself why I was doing it, and I'm sure Barry has asked himself the same question. Poker books are normally written by players who hope to make more money selling books than they can playing poker. Barry and I each gave up a substantial amount of money we probably would have made playing poker while we were working on our books instead. We can never recoup that money from book sales. And for what reason? So we could help our opponents become better players? We must be sick.

I have had the dubious honor of getting knocked out of a tournament by a younger player who thanked me for improving his game. And then, before I could make my exit from the table, he asked for my autograph. Well, now I will be able to laugh when it happens to Barry.

Doyle Brunson
Las Vegas, Nevada
May 2005

Introduction

When I was in college in the early 1970s, I read every poker book I could get my hands on. Some contained amusing anecdotes, but they didn't teach me to play poker. Most books written after 1975 have done a good job of comparing starting hands in different forms of poker. Also, many of them include useful advice for play on early betting rounds.

This book does not contain charts on starting hand requirements, since my basic strategy is not significantly different from that which you would find in other books. If I told you those differences, it would be of little value, except for playing against me.

Most current poker books were written by middle-limit players or players who have had some tournament success. Their advice is worthwhile for beginning and intermediate players, but is often invalid for players who make a living playing poker. In contrast, this book contains material for professional poker players and those aspiring to become professionals.

Though I have tried to arrange the topics in a logical order, I believe each chapter can be read independently. I start with the story of my poker career which contains hints of lessons that will be presented in later chapters. After describing the poker world, I discuss philosophies that have helped me, and I also touch on some social commentary. Next are advanced topics, including poker instruction and my analyses of several key hands I played in prestigious tournaments.

A good poker player must adjust to his opponents' overall strategies and to specific plays revealed by their mannerisms. To be successful, he must also manage his life well. While it is not possible to excel at poker without devoting time to playing and to analyzing problems that arise, I hope this book will help players improve in less time than it would take them on their own.

Many assertions in the book are not based on scientific study or mathematical proof. They are only the results of my observations. However, I did write computer programs to verify some of the material. These programs and other information can be found on my website at *barrygreenstein.com*. I believe this book contains enough thought-provoking material so even readers with little interest in playing high-stakes poker will find lessons that apply to a variety of situations. The Glossary may be helpful to those who are unfamiliar with poker terms.

Barry Greenstein
Rancho Palos Verdes, California
April 2005

PART I

Chapter 1

My Poker Career

"Life can only be understood backwards; but it must be lived forwards."

Soren Kierkegaard (1813 – 1855), Danish writer and philosopher

Ace on the River

When I was four years old, I asked my father about the purpose of the plastic chips that were in a cylindrical holder on a table in our dining room. He told me they were for a game called poker which he had played in the army during World War II. He took a deck of cards out of the holder and dealt each of us five cards face down. He was showing me a version of poker called five-card draw. He said I could throw away any cards I didn't want and I would be dealt other cards to replace them. The object of the game, he explained, was to get the best hand according to a chart that came with the deck of cards.

"But what about the chips?" I asked. "Those are for betting," he replied. "The better your hand is, the more you bet. The people you're playing against can match your bet or just drop out. Sometimes you can bet with a bad hand and try to scare people into dropping out. That's called bluffing."

At home we often played the board games Clue, Scrabble, Sorry, and Monopoly, but I preferred playing canasta and gin rummy with my mother. However, by the time I was in fifth grade, I stopped playing cards with

her, so she played gin rummy with my brother Howie who is four years younger than I am.

One time, as I was watched them play, I noticed that my mom held "gin" in her hand but didn't put it down. I could see that she was letting my brother win. I said, "Mom, you're cheating." She put her finger to her lips and whispered, "Shhhh. Do you think I didn't do that for you?" I now realize that the confidence I have today is partly due to my mother letting me win when I was a child.

My Poker Career

I played in my first organized poker game when I was twelve years old. We must have been playing for quarters, because I remember those quarters jumping in my pockets as I was chased by an unhappy sixteen year old opponent who seemed intent on getting the $24 I had won. Later, when I was going to high school, I played poker on weekend nights for dollars. Although I usually won, I didn't hold on to a lot of money. I spent freely and lost some of the money shooting pool.

I have been a very successful poker player, but it has not been easy. I have been broke at times, either because of bad spending habits or just because of the natural ups and downs of the game. Poker playing is not a career that offers a smooth ride to the top. Many poker players are regularly broke, enjoying only brief spells in which they have money and no outstanding debts. A very small percentage of players make a net profit.

In addition to poker, I gambled on golf, but all the money would go back into the game in the form of greens fees and other expenses. One of my biggest disadvantages in playing golf and shooting pool was honesty: if I lost I paid, but I didn't always get paid if I won. At least when you're

playing poker, the money is there in the form of chips or cash.

By the time I was 18 and a sophomore in college, I had built up a bankroll of about $1500. More than 30 years ago this was a lot of money. A semester's in-state tuition at the University of Illinois was $300. In the game I'd been playing, $100 or $200 was a decent-sized win. One day I heard there was a bigger game in Danville, a town about 25 miles from Champaign, Illinois. It was no-limit hold'em, my best game, and I was eager to try it. Someone gave me a ride and we got to the game around 7 p.m.

Ace on the River

I had been playing very conservatively for a few hours and was about $200 ahead when the following hand came up. I had all my money on the table, and I was dealt two Queens. The flop came K-Q-2 with two hearts. I called a bet on the flop. An offsuit Three came on the turn and a player named Bob Slinker bet about $300. That's when I moved in for the rest of my chips. A third player had only about $100 left, and he called. Now Slinker had to think. Everyone knew I was playing very tight. But while Slinker was trying to decide what to do, the dealer burned and turned. He didn't realize that Slinker hadn't called my bet! A black card was dealt. Slinker flashed his cards — the Ace-King of hearts — and said, "It's almost impossible to fold this hand, but I think you have a set." He had top pair and a flush draw, and he finally decided to call. Two other players whispered that they had each thrown away two hearts.

Since the dealer had mistakenly dealt the river, there had to be a ruling about what to do next. In most places, the dealer would just burn and turn again. In some, the mistakenly dealt card would be shuffled in first. But in this house game, they did something I've never seen anywhere to this day. Their rule was to burn the same number of cards as there were players in the pot. So the dealer burned two cards. The new river card was the Eight of hearts, which was devastating for me.

It was about one o'clock in the morning, and I had lost all the money I had saved. A player turned over the deck and the burned cards. The Eight was the only heart left in the deck.

I didn't know how I was going to get home. The friend who had given me a ride lived in Danville, and he wasn't going back to Champaign. No one else was about to quit and the game would probably go on through the night. I left the house, and after walking three miles, I came to a river with a bridge over it. I remember thinking to myself, "Someone else might jump off this bridge right now. But no one can do that to me." When I got to the expressway, I tried to hitchhike but nobody picked me up. I walked for five hours. I saw the sun come up. My friend from the game called me the next day. He said the dealer had made another mistake. The dealer had forgotten about the third player in the hand who was all-in. He should have burned three cards, not two.

I always remember that as the worst hand of my life. It symbolizes that everything can go wrong and things could always be worse.

When I was 20, my roommate told me poker was legal in California and persuaded me to go there with him. We flew to L.A. and went down to nearby Gardena, where there were six cardrooms at the time. Before we checked into our hotel, I went down to one of the cardrooms because I still didn't believe poker was really legal there. I wanted to see it for myself.

The cardrooms were legal all right, but hold'em was illegal. However, high and low draw poker were legal. Thick cigarette smoke filled the room from about neck-high all the way to the ceiling. I thought, "How can people play in these conditions?" My roommate told me, "I always throw up right after I leave."

I put myself on a schedule. I would sleep until 5 p.m., go to the cardroom at 6, and play until the club closed at 2 a.m. I won consistently and thought it must be because I was the best player. But that wasn't the reason. I was playing against people who had worked all day and had a few drinks to relax. Meanwhile, I was resting and training for the event. I didn't know the difference until I got a job and tried to play after working all day. I was a basket case. On that trip to California, I didn't win because I was a better player. I won because of my preparation.

During finals week of my senior year in college, the poker games were especially good. I knew that if I got an A in my chemistry course I would graduate with "highest honors," whereas if I got a B, I'd only get "high honors." I needed a high grade on the chemistry final exam to get an A in the course. I had to decide whether to study for the final or play poker. I decided I'd rather play poker. I got a C on the exam and a B in the course. I found out later that I would have received an A in the course if I'd just gotten a B on that final, as it was graded on a curve. I was so angry at myself for putting poker first that I threw out my "high honors" diploma.

I graduated from college in three years with a degree in computer science and spent another ten years in graduate school studying mathematics. I found poker games in cities in the area — Champaign, Urbana, Decatur, Danville — and in small towns in Illinois and sometimes Indiana. I could find somewhere to play almost every night. A few times, I flew to Houston, Texas, because I could play in bigger games there. As I continued to win, I played for higher stakes. I had started playing poker for quarters at age twelve. In high school I played for dollars, and in college I often won hundreds of dollars. By the time I graduated from college, I could win $1000 on a good night. When I was in graduate school, I could win a few thousand dollars in a session.

To find players, I took out advertisements in the school newspaper, offering to give poker lessons. Someone would call me and say, "Who are you to give lessons? I know how to play poker." Or some would ask, "What's the charge?" I'd say, "You just have to play against me. I get to keep what you lose, and I'll tell you what you did wrong." I even played with a few professors. It was embarrassing for them because I was always the better player, and they didn't want anyone to find out.

We sometimes played a game called Black Mariah, a version of stud in which the player with the high spade in the hole splits the pot with the high hand. One player, Darryl, often ended up with the Ace of spades in the hole whenever he dealt that game. We all knew it and we'd just fold. As long as we didn't play his game, he couldn't win. One night, a couple of grad students who had answered my ad in the paper joined the game. I told them, "Don't play on Darryl's deal." Although he had been warned, one of the new players couldn't resist playing his two black Kings in the hole. He lost to Darryl's two black Aces. I took him aside and said, "I told you so."

The player who lost with the Kings was furious. He called the police the next day, and somehow the FBI got involved. The FBI agents were very thorough. They came to my apartment where the game was held and talked to me. They knew all the players' names and other details of the game, and said, "We hear you're harboring a cheat." They told me they didn't normally bust poker games unless there was violence or the wives complained. "But you've got students in the game, and we don't want to deal with their parents." So from then on, I didn't allow any students in the game unless I was sure they could be trusted.

Meanwhile, Darryl realized we were onto him and accused *us* of cheating *him*. One night, he wrote checks totaling about $3000 for his losses, and he called the next day to say he'd stopped payment on the checks. It was a Saturday, and in those days banks weren't open on weekends. The players to whom Darryl had written checks went to the bank as soon as it opened on Monday morning. It turned out that Darryl had only about $2800 in the bank, so to be able to cash all the checks, they made a $200 deposit. They came back to town and triumphantly told the story. When Darryl found out what had happened, he sued for triple damages, which amounted to $8400. Unfortunately, gambling debts aren't legally collectable in Illinois. The other players settled out of court, and Darryl ended up getting about $1800 back.

Around that time, two players who ran a poker game used the rake to buy a house for the game. It was a nice four-bedroom house in a small town, and anyone could use it or take girls there on the off nights. We played in the basement. One night, three or four guys came down the stairs with guns drawn. I was terrified when I saw the barrel of a gun pointed at me, but then the nicest word I've ever heard came out of the first guy's mouth: "Police." I've never been so happy to hear that word. If it hadn't been the police, it might have been a very ugly situation. They confiscated all the money. I had the most, about $10,000, because someone had paid me some money he owed me. All together, the police collected about $30,000 in cash.

I asked the police if they had a warrant, and one of them showed it to me. The judge who signed it was a friend of mine. I said, "I know that judge. He'd never sign that warrant." We played the card game hearts for money in Champaign every Wednesday night. He knew about the poker game, and I couldn't imagine him signing a warrant to bust it. But there was nothing we could do, and the cops hauled us in. Since I had the most money, they thought I was the kingpin. I called my girlfriend Joyce and told her to bring some hundreds out of the drawer for bail. When the police saw her with the wad of $100 bills, they thought we were Bonnie and Clyde. Joyce bailed everyone out.

The next day I saw my friend the judge. "Bob, how could you sign that warrant?" I asked. "That was your poker game? They told me it was a casino!" he exclaimed. It turned out that the judge in the town where the game was held was a friend of some of the players and he refused to sign the warrant. So the police went to Bob and lied to him. They said the other judge was out of town and they needed Bob's help to bust an illegal casino. That's why he signed the warrant.

One of the players who was a respected trial attorney vowed to fight the case. He was convinced that it was legal to play poker in the privacy of one's home and we could win in court. But that was the last thing the sheriff's office wanted. The news that the sheriff had busted a casino, after staking it out for months and confiscating so much money, was all over the papers. The sheriff said, "Don't go to court. I'll return your money after the election." And that's exactly what happened.

When I was about 22, I went to Las Vegas and played razz — seven-card stud for low — at the Stardust. One player took me aside and said, "I can see you're a good poker player. Want to be on our team?" I replied, "I'm not interested in being on a team." He said, "You don't get it. We're trying to beat the tourists, not each other. Don't fight us."

Everyone in Vegas was hustling. I played with a nice old woman who said she was just learning the game and waiting for her husband. I won a big pot and suddenly she turned into a different person. Her face was red with anger and she said, "Sonny, I've been playing poker since before your parents even thought about having you."

The last straw was when I sat down in the $20-$40 seven-card stud game, the biggest game there. It was an eight-handed game, and before a hand was dealt a friend of mine said, "Those are some of the best players in Vegas. I don't think you should play." I got up and told them not to deal me in, and one of the other players remarked, "Well then, there's no reason to deal." That was when I decided not to play poker in Las Vegas. I thought, "I make a good living playing poker in Illinois. I don't need this."

My Poker Career

When I decided not to play in Vegas, I meant it. In 1978, my home game in Illinois held a "satellite" tournament for the *World Series of Poker*. Ten people put up $1000 each, and the winner would earn a $10,000 seat at the Series. I warned them that if I won I'd just take the money, because I refused to play poker in Vegas. I did win and did take the money, so our game didn't have a representative at the World Series.

Around 1979, Larry Parker, a friend of mine who ran a poker game in Decatur, Illinois, moved to Houston and invited me to come there. He told me they had good no-limit games, but they didn't always let good players play. However, he could get me in. It also helped that I never claimed to be a professional poker player. They called me "the perfessor" since I had mentioned teaching students at the University of Illinois. (I taught for several years while I was doing my graduate work.) The predominant games in Houston were no-limit hold'em, lowball, and Juarez — a game similar to Omaha but with three hole cards instead of four. That gave me experience with Omaha-type games before the game of Omaha existed.

In Houston, cardrooms were legal as long as they were private clubs and gave some money to charity. When I was there, poker legend Jack Straus was playing at the Redmen's Club. The game had a $1000 buy-in and he bought in for $5000. Meanwhile, a guy in his twenties was trying to sell his wife's jewelry because he wanted to play in the game. He said the jewelry was worth $20,000, but he would sell it for $10,000 to get a stake. No one was interested in buying it.

I sat down to play with Straus, who was an extremely aggressive player. He was so aggressive that every time I had a hand I'd just check and let him bet. He'd bet on the flop, the turn, and the river. I called him on the river at least three times and he was bluffing each time. After a while, I had beaten Straus out of $15,000. He called over the guy with the jewelry and said, "Hey kid, I don't want your wife's jewelry. Here's $10,000. Get my money back. There's a bigger game I have to go to in San Antonio."

Another player my friend Larry introduced to me was Joe Hodges. Joe was a compulsive gambler who had even written a book called *Compulsion*. I saw him a couple of years later in Las Vegas. I was there to play blackjack, and Joe was attending a convention of the American Medical Association. A psychiatrist had been going on talk shows to tell about his revolutionary method for curing compulsive gamblers, and Joe was his Exhibit A. But Joe wasn't cured. He was still a compulsive gambler.

Ace on the River

During that trip, Joe didn't want the doctors to see him gamble, so he tried to get his friends to place bets for him. One night we went out together to shoot dice. I usually just bet on six and eight, but I was trying to show off, so I bet larger amounts and on more numbers than usual — four and ten as well as six and eight. The shooter rolled a nine, which meant he had to roll another nine before he rolled a seven, for me to win. Joe said, "I can't believe you're doing this." I couldn't figure out what he was talking about. I thought, "I'm betting twice as much money on twice as many numbers as I usually do." In my mind, I was gambling like a wild man. Then Joe said, "Aren't you afraid he's going to roll a five?" Five was the only number I didn't have a bet on.

That taught me a lesson about compulsive gambling. A compulsive gambler is afraid to miss a potential winning action. When he sees a sporting event on television, he thinks, "Someone has to win. I just have to pick the right side." Conversely, when I am aware of a good poker game, I sometimes decide that it is more important to spend time with my family. In other words, I try to be rational rather than compulsive.

Around this time, the game in which I played in Illinois consisted mainly of local farmers and businessmen. A good win in that game was $5000 to $10,000. Often when there was a big pot, someone would say, "Boy, you could buy a new Cadillac with that money." After I won a pot from one of the farmers, he said to me, "I was going to take my family on a trip this weekend, but now I guess we can't go." I felt terrible.

In the mid-1970s, many American farmers were going through a recession. I was about 26 years old, and I didn't need these people's money nearly as much as they did. I had plenty of money, over $100,000, and decided to give them a break. I stopped playing poker for a while and went back to working on my Ph.D. thesis.

In 1984, I moved to California with my wife Donna, whom I had met on the tournament bridge circuit. We wanted to get custody of her three children from a previous marriage, and our lawyer said we wouldn't have much of a chance if my occupation was listed as "professional gambler," so I took a job at a software company which later became known as Symantec.

My Poker Career

The timing was bad for me because I needed only a few months to finish the final edits for my Ph.D. thesis.

Part of the reason I took the job was that it was near the Cameo Club cardroom in Palo Alto. I thought I could play poker in my spare time, since by my standards, the programming job didn't pay enough. I didn't think I'd keep the job long — just until I won the court case. But Symantec was a start-up company, and I got involved in a project writing the product Q & A. This prevented me from taking the break I needed to finish typing my Ph.D. thesis. During this period my wife would call me at work and say, "What are you doing? There are good poker games here!"

In the San Jose/San Francisco Bay Area where I lived, hold'em was illegal at that time. The game that was almost exclusively played was no-limit lowball, and the biggest game had a $3000 buy-in. The second-biggest game had a $200 buy-in. I had played in games comparable to the biggest game, but I wanted to be careful. I was working full-time for around $40,000 a year, which meant I could lose a year's salary in the big game after only a few losses. But my wife wanted me to play in the biggest game, because she had always seen me win at poker. I said, "If I ever win $3000 in the second-biggest game, I'll use it to play in the biggest game."

Ace on the River

We had trouble supporting our lifestyle and family with my paycheck, but I was a key employee at Symantec and felt obligated to stay. At one time, Donna and I could come up with only $40. Donna went to a $20 buy-in game and built it up to about $300. Then I took it to the $200 buy-in game, and within a month I had a $3000 win and used it to enter the biggest game.

By that time, I had been playing in the second-biggest game for almost a year. When I graduated to the biggest game, they never knew what hit them. Two of the self-proclaimed best players were broke within a year. But if I had tried to play in the biggest game right away, they would have beaten me. I wasn't as good as I thought I was, and they were experts at that particular game. That year I spent in the second-biggest game was the apprenticeship I needed to beat the big game.

For a long stretch while I lived in the Bay Area, I played hardly any poker at all. I didn't have time. I threw myself into the word processing program I was working on for Symantec, perhaps because I had never finished my Ph.D. and I wanted to prove I could see a project through to completion. I worked seventeen hours a day, seven days a week. I would go home, sleep, and go right back to work. In 1985, I worked so hard that the only break I took was at 9:30 p.m. on the Fourth of July. I went up to the roof of the building and watched the fireworks for 15 minutes.

When I did go back to playing poker, Donna and I started to have disagreements about money. If I won $10,000, then lost $5000, I thought I was up $5000. Donna thought I was down $5000 because we already had the $10,000. However, during our divorce proceedings, her lawyer said a figure of plus $10,000 should be used in the calculation of my income because the $5000 loss was a result of my gambling problem. Apparently there were three possible answers to 10 minus 5.

I was cheated twice that I know of at the Cameo Club — once with marked cards for a period of a couple of months, and the second time by a player named Rick Riolo with a set-up involving cameras. It was an inside job, with the manager of the club reading people's cards with infrared cameras and communicating with Rick and another player through speakers in their ears. But Rick's partner, who liked me, said, "You don't want to play in this game." After a couple of losses, I understood what he was trying to tell me and I quit. It helped that Rick's partner considered me to be a nice person and tipped me off. It also helped that I had been cheated before, so when I was losing and thought I should be winning, I was more alert.

My Poker Career

In 1988, hold'em was finally legalized in California. My wife and daughter were suffering from expensive and time-consuming health problems, and I knew I was going to have to quit Symantec and go back to playing poker to support my family. I finally stopped working at Symantec in 1990. Being in California all those years turned out to be an advantage. Vegas pros would come to California to play, and they had no idea who I was. They'd never seen me before and thought I was a local businessman. They certainly didn't know that no-limit hold'em was my best game.

Since hold'em was a new game in California and a lot of the players only knew lowball, I became a sort of mentor for the whole area. People at various clubs watched me play and started to understand how to bet their hands. A surprising consequence of this was revealed when Diego Cordovez won a bracelet in no-limit hold'em at the 2000 *World Series of Poker*. I was playing in a side game at the Horseshoe, and within minutes after he won, Diego came up to me and said, "I couldn't have won this without you." I didn't remember ever playing with him. He must have watched me play without me being aware of it.

But the no-limit games eventually dried up, and I had to do something I never thought I'd do — play limit hold'em. To me, it was like watching paint dry. I had to play twelve hours a day, seven days a week, just to make ends meet. Initially, I played in the $30-$60 game because I didn't understand limit poker well enough to play in the biggest game, which was $80-$160. I jumped up to $80-$160 only when I knew weak players were there. As I had done before with lowball, I went through an apprenticeship in the smaller game and learned by watching better players and asking questions. It probably took me six months before I felt comfortable in the biggest limit game.

In 1992, I finally decided to try the final event at the *World Series of Poker*. Through the luck of the draw, my starting table was full of well-known pros, including Johnny Chan, Erik Seidel, Bobby Hoff, Carl McKelvey, Paul "Eskimo" Clark, and Dewey Tomko. Many people said it was the toughest table they had ever seen. In most people's eyes, I was the only weak spot.

At the end of the first day, I had more chips than anyone else at our table. A bookie named Terry Rogers, who was making odds on the tournament, had made me 100 to 1 against winning. At the beginning of the second day, he came up to me and said, "If you win, it's going to bust me. I don't know who you are, but a lot of the best players are putting their money on you."

I came in 22nd and won $8100, which meant I actually lost $1900 of the $10,000 buy-in. I was so disappointed that I went across the street to the Golden Nugget and within 20 minutes had lost the entire $8100 playing blackjack. I went home with no money in my pocket.

But when I went to the Cameo Club, there was a banner on the wall: "Congratulations Barry!" No one from the club had ever done that well

in the World Series. I thought, "I have no money in my pocket, and they want to throw me a party?"

Around that time I found out I was being investigated by the IRS. I met with the investigator and said, "I pay my taxes. What's the problem?" He told me I was guilty of structuring, a serious crime. Structuring is when you deposit, for example, $9000 in the bank twice to avoid having to fill out a Currency Transaction Report, which you have to do for any cash deposit over $10,000. The IRS agent asked me why the club couldn't just write me a check. The reason was that if I had a losing day, I would write a personal check to the club, often for more money than I had in the bank. The next morning I would take cash, sometimes borrowed, to deposit in the bank so that my personal check wouldn't bounce.

The agent and I came to an agreement. If I could, I would deposit at least $10,000 and declare it to make it clear that I wasn't hiding anything. If I didn't need to put cash in my account to make the funds immediately available to cover a personal check, I'd get a check from the club. They've never bothered me since.

At that time, I would often play all night, trying to win enough money to pay my mortgage and meet all my expenses. When the dealers came in for a new shift at 6:00 a.m., I was often still there with a lot of chips on the table, waiting until I had to take my kids to school at 7:00. They'd always ask, "Boy, how much do you need to get even?" After a while, I started taking some of my chips off the table so they would think I was losing like everyone else who had played all night.

It was at about this time that I met Mimi Tran, a beautiful Vietnamese

woman who was hanging around the small games. We struck a deal: I would teach her poker if she would teach me Vietnamese. We would go for long drives teaching each other. When we first met, her English wasn't very good, so I didn't realize how intelligent she was. But it turned out that she had a phenomenal memory. She could go through every hand she had played in a session and tell me exactly what she did. Under my tutelage, she moved up quickly from $3-$6 to $6-$12, then $15-$30, and sometimes into a really good $30-$60 game.

When I first started giving Mimi poker lessons, I said I would only teach her with this stipulation: "If I tell you to quit for the day, you have to quit. If you play under the wrong conditions, you're going to be a losing player. This is a lifetime agreement, no matter what happens between us." She didn't really buy it, but she agreed. Initially, she thought I was just a rich guy who liked to gamble. She didn't believe anyone really made a living that way. But when she started playing and realized that what I told her really worked, she began to believe me. From that point on she won consistently, and as she didn't spend money like I did, I was soon borrowing money from her. People thought Mimi had a sugar daddy — in fact, the opposite was true. Once, when she graduated to the $80-$160

game, we both went through a really good stretch and each won about $100,000. She asked, "How much do you have left?" I said, "About $5000, and you?" She had about $95,000.

Then we had a problem: there was only one $80-$160 game. We tried to play in alternating shifts, but sometimes we'd both want to play, and when we did that, people complained that we might be partners. Eventually, I flew down to Los Angeles to play poker in the casinos in that area. The nice thing I found when I got there was that not only were there bigger games, but they were mixed games — limit and no-limit, lowball and hold'em and so on, all at one table. It was perfect for me. I did extremely well, and once again I seemed to come out of nowhere. This occurred around 1994.

A few years later, I was invited to play stud at Larry Flynt's house, a $1500-$3000 game. Some top players were excluded. Even though some players considered me to be a top player, others held on to the perception that I was very wealthy as a result of my time at Symantec. This persona helped me get invited, since wealthy non-professional players are the most sought-after opponents. The stakes in the Flynt game were higher than I was used to playing. The biggest regular game I had played in before that was about $400-$800. Another problem was that they played seven-card stud, a game I had hardly played since I was a kid. I won the first five times I played, for a total of about $250,000. After a few sessions, the other players caught on to some of my tendencies. I lost more than I had originally won and had to borrow from Mimi to stay in the game.

I would occasionally play smaller stakes seven-card stud for practice, and I would often analyze my play later. I also read material on seven-card stud, the most helpful being Chip Reese's section in Doyle Brunson's *Super/System* book. We played about three times a week. It took three years for me to consider myself a good stud player. One factor that made a big difference was my decision to move to L.A. Before, when I was flying there and back to San Jose all the time, I was always tired, sometimes even falling asleep at the table. Especially in stud, where you have to assimilate a lot of information, that's not good. If I hadn't moved, I would have gone broke, because everyone's game was improving — not just mine — and weaker players were dropping out. But once I moved to L.A., the tables were turned as I now had home-court advantage over those who continued to fly in.

Ted Forrest, an experienced stud player, got into the game and started to beat it. He seemed to play worse hands than other players, but he bet them better and won consistently. People thought he was just very lucky. I observed how he played and learned from him. Whenever someone is beating a game consistently, the other players will always complain about how lucky that person is. They won't give him credit for outplaying them. I try to observe those "lucky" players and figure out how they make their opponents play badly against them.

Despite consistently beating the game, my spending habits still caused the money to disappear. I rarely left myself enough money to lose three times in a row. I wasn't broke — I had plenty of assets — but I was cash-poor, and I would have to liquidate something if I experienced a losing streak. If I had to, I would write markers at various casinos. I also had an arrangement with a bookie. I would pay him $25,000 a week when I lost betting sports with him, and he would give me the money he owed me if I won. The bookie didn't mind if I owed him money because he knew I would continue betting as I tried to get even. I once lost $500,000 in a single month. Meanwhile, Ted Forrest and I played Chinese poker after the stud games. Over a period of a month and a half, I had lost $1.5 million.

I didn't have the money. I had recently suffered substantial losses in the stock market. I owed the bookie and I wrote markers at the casinos to my maximum credit limit. I looked out of my window at a piece of property I had intended to buy and told myself, "Well, you can't buy it now."

Playing Chinese poker was an especially stupid idea. I thought I had an edge, but if I did it was no more than one-tenth of one percent. Furthermore, I would stay up all night, and the next day I'd have to miss the poker game, or if I played I would be too tired to play well. It wasn't worth it.

By then I had been contributing for a few years to an international charity called Children, Incorporated. One of the group's coordinators said to me, "You must be a wealthy man." I thought about it and said,

My Poker Career

"Actually, I'm a negative millionaire, but giving $1000 away has no impact on my financial situation." At my lowest point, I owed $1.1 million.

Several people who played in the big stud game had, at one time, been ahead more than a million dollars, but I was the only professional player who was able to continue playing through the seven years that the game was going on. The others were careless with the money they made or got into a losing streak they couldn't play through.

Meanwhile, I had abandoned my boycott of Las Vegas. From my observation, management in the poker rooms in Las Vegas had become much more involved in ensuring the integrity of the games than they had been in the 1970s. Actually, I had started playing occasionally in Las Vegas again in 1991, when the big hold'em game in the Bay Area broke down. At that time, people told me I should play with Chip Reese and Doyle Brunson, the most legendary players in Vegas, because they would not expect someone they had never heard of to be very good. I said, "Nah,

I'm not playing to boost my ego, and besides, I heard they're partners." But two players, Bobby Hoff and Carl McKelvey, gave me $20,000 to play in the game. I put in $10,000 of my own, giving us a bankroll of $30,000. I had never given anyone a piece of my action, but I reluctantly decided to play in the game with Chip and Doyle.

When I arrived at the casino, I saw there was a $5000 buy-in game with several weak players whom I recognized, including one whose nickname was Precious. I said, "Why should I go up against the best players when there's a juicy smaller game right here?" I convinced my partners that it would be smarter if I played in the smaller game. I bought in for $5000 five times and Precious busted me each time. After Precious beat me out of $25,000, he quit and the game broke up. Even though I lost, I am still confident that my decision to play in the smaller game was correct. That's the only time I've ever had a partner.

Years later, when I finally took a shot at the bigger game, Chip and Doyle were extremely nice to me. I came to realize that great players are usually nice to new players. They don't win by cheating, but by getting people involved. A good gambler gets people to gamble with him and finds

situations where he can beat them out of their money. In the course of playing with them, it also became obvious to me that Chip and Doyle were not partners, but were friendly rivals.

In April 2001, I first played in the biggest game in Vegas with Chip, Doyle, Lyle Berman, Bobby Baldwin, Chau Giang, and a rotating cast of about ten others. The game was $4000-$8000 limit, mixed with pot-limit Omaha and no-limit Deuce-to-Seven lowball. I did well and won several hundred thousand dollars over about ten sessions. The following year I brought about $200,000 to Vegas to play in the game again, but they'd moved the limits up to $8,000-$16,000, and that was just too big. I decided to play in smaller games instead.

In 2003, during the *World Series of Poker*, the game was cut back down to $4000-$8000. I got off to a good start and never looked back. I beat the game badly and won several million dollars. Once again, a good rest schedule was my biggest asset. When I was losing, I quit and went to bed

because I knew there would still be a big game the next day. I had planned to go home and see my kids, but I flew them out to be with me instead. I didn't want to miss the game and take the pressure off my opponents. I wanted to keep them on the run. In addition to outmanaging my opponents, I had my family backing me up. My partner Alexandra was traveling back and forth between L.A. and Las Vegas taking care of the kids and me. I talked to my kids once or twice a day and told them it was important that they behave and do their homework so I could be successful at my job.

In March of 2003, eight players entered a winner-take-all $125,000 buy-in seven-card stud tournament at Larry Flynt's Hustler Casino. Larry asked the players to agree not to make any deals to split the prize money when it got down to two players, so he could say that the first prize was $1,000,000. I quickly agreed since I wanted to play for the full million. But Doyle Brunson said it was unreasonable for Larry to tell people what to do with their own money, and from his experience there was no way to stop people from making a private deal. As luck would have it, Larry and I were the final two players. At this point Larry said to me, "Let's make a deal. You keep the chips in front of you and I'll keep mine." I said, "Larry, I promised you I wouldn't make a deal." He responded, "Doyle said people always make deals." I play with Larry often and I knew he would enjoy coming in second place and making a profit from his own tournament.

He was proud to have outlasted Johnny Chan, Ted Forrest, Doyle Brunson, Steve Wolff, Jerry Buss, and Phil Ivey. Since Larry and I are friends, we agreed to play one hour heads-up, and at the end of the hour my share was $770,000. Subtracting my entry and tip, this left me with a profit of $609,000.

With part of my winnings, I bought sports cars for my brother and sister. I decided to give the rest of the money to people who help other

people. In this way, I could leverage the giving. I had visited some children I sponsored through Children, Incorporated and I remembered how dedicated the coordinators were. Those I came in contact with lived in lower-income areas, often worked unpaid overtime, and used their own resources to help underprivileged children. I gave $1000 to each of the 440 coordinators around the world. Their letters, indicating in detail what they had done with the money, were the most heartwarming "thank-you's" I have ever received.

I finally had a reason to play in tournaments. I thought it would be easier for people to accept my money if they felt they were sharing my tournament wins. Also, the media exposure would encourage others to contribute as well. I had previously hidden my profession from people involved in my charitable causes, because I thought they might consider my money "dirty." But tournament poker is more like a sport or the lottery, and people were glad to share the gains from my winnings. I feel fortunate that I am in a financial position to do this. Many poker players have told me they wish they could do the same thing. I tell them I took care of my family first, and now I am able to help others. I believe most poker players are generous — partly due to their lack of respect for money — and I feel as if I am carrying the flag for those who have not been as successful as I have.

In the past year and a half, I have won seven tournaments and come in second five times. I have won and donated about three million dollars from poker tournaments. There has been a lot of press coverage for the charities to which I contribute, and this has helped them considerably. I have been given an extremely positive persona by the media, but I find it amusing to read some of the negative comments. One tongue-in-cheek response was, "The money is gone forever from the poker economy, squandered on starving children throughout the world. Well, maybe they will grow up to be poker players."

People assume that since I have given away a few million dollars, I must be worth hundreds of millions. Even though I was only a programmer at Symantec, I have often read that I founded the company and sold it for millions or even billions of dollars. One of my favorite quotes is "Gee, the guy is worth a billion and he donates a million. Kinda like me dropping a quarter in that drunk homeless guy's McDonald's cup." I have also been called a filthy-rich guy who gives away money he can well afford for his self-promotion. I admit that I have had an increase in self-esteem as a result of the donations, but I only wanted attention drawn to the charities so more people would follow my example. Many poker players have sponsored children as a result of my efforts.

I have seen posts on the Internet insinuating I am doing this for a tax deduction, as if this were an old car whose value I was overstating. Maybe these people don't realize that I have to declare tournament winnings as income before I start taking deductions. Actually, the government allows only 25% of one's income to be declared as charity. Consequently, if I don't make any other money, I have to pay taxes on 75% of the tournament winnings even though I have given that money away. I hope to be able to make enough in the side games so I can deduct all that I give away, but my increased participation in tournaments has limited my side-game play. It is likely that I will have to cut back on my charitable contributions in the future. Otherwise, I will not be able to afford the taxes.

I have heard claims that I win tournaments because some people, influenced by my cause, play "soft" against me. Several times when I have made a bet, my opponents have folded and said that they know I give the money to charity so they are going to let me win the pot. I suspect they first decided to fold and then used that line as a cover-up, in case they made the wrong play. Name players like me wear a bull's-eye on their back, and other players are happy to brag about knocking one of us out of a big tournament. I have even been accused of donating money to charity as a scam to increase my positive karma. When I win a pot with an inferior hand I have heard people say, "God is on his side."

I frequently get calls from tournament promoters and representatives of online sites telling me that if I endorse their venture, part of the proceeds will go to my charitable causes. When I turn down the "win-win" proposal, as they often call it, they never seem to understand. I translate it to mean, "We want to use your causes to make money for us." If people want to give money to charity, let them do it. I am never going to tell anyone to gamble to help poor children.

The overwhelming response I have received about my charitable work has, of course, been very positive. When I walk through a card room, many people shake my hand and compliment me. I can invariably get reservations at hotels, restaurants, and entertainment events even when they are supposedly sold out. I can't deny that the attention I get is very gratifying, but I try to keep it in perspective. I don't pretend to be Mother Theresa.

Ace on the River

Meanwhile, Doyle Brunson asked me to write a chapter for the sequel to his landmark book, *Super/System*. I told him I could write about how to make money at poker as I felt this would be a good complement to the technical material in his book. Doyle wanted about twenty pages, but my manuscript escalated to over one hundred. I asked him which part he would like to use, and he replied, "It's all good. I wouldn't want to cut out any of it." He gave me a choice: either write a shortened version or make a book out of it for myself. As I had already spent a lot of time on this project, I decided to choose the latter. This book is the result.

MY POKER STATISTICS

I have played poker for a living since 1968. When I played no-limit, I won more than 75% of my sessions. When I played limit, I won around 58% of my sessions. Until 1997, I averaged less than one losing month per year. In 1997, I started playing in a high-stakes game that is played a couple of times per week. I averaged four losing months per year for the first six years of the game, and I have won only about 50% of the sessions.

My average win has been much larger than my average loss. It may seem that I have achieved success by quitting when I was losing and playing when I was winning to account for this disparity. In reality, I have played to the end of almost every session. It is not my control, but rather my opponents' lack of control, that has contributed to these results.

I have spent extravagantly and made all the mistakes that are mentioned in this book except for using alcohol and drugs. I have often been in a position where I would be broke or at least short of cash if I have one bad month. Currently, I am in very good financial shape, but there are no guarantees I will stay this way since I am always involved in many personal and philanthropic projects.

CHAPTER 2

THE POKER SOCIETY

"All the world's a stage, and all the men and women merely players."

Jaques, in As You Like It by William Shakespeare (1564-1616), English playwright

Ace on the River

MANY OF THE CHARACTERS IN THE POKER SOCIETY ARE NOT FOUND IN OTHER ENVIRONMENTS.

CASINO PERSONNEL

Casino executives. The majority of casino owners and executives view players as if they are sick gamblers. The predominant stance is "If we build it, they will come." They want to maximize profits from every part of the casino. They usually don't understand how all the pieces fit together, and they don't have the tools to evaluate which ideas generate revenue.

The following employees should be tipped and complimented for their good service. An extra tip around the holiday season is deserved and pragmatic.

Floorpeople/hosts. They can supply you with information about good games. If you give them your phone number, they can contact you when a live one is playing or, more importantly, when he is planning to play. An advance call may prevent you from being locked out.

Cage people. In many casinos, people in the cashier's cage, especially cage supervisors, are more influential than you might think. They may have authority to cash checks and hold markers. Over the course of time, you may have opportunities to correct mistakes made in your favor, thus demonstrating that you are an honest person.

Waiters/Waitresses, porters, and chip runners. They are the working class of the casino. Tip them accordingly,

and don't take out your frustration on them when you are losing. They are your connection with humanity.

Dealers. They are just the messengers of poker hands, but are often blamed for the message.

Security. They are the lifeguards in the casino. It doesn't hurt to have them looking after you.

Tournament staff. This group was formerly like a traveling circus, but now that tournaments are proven revenue generators, they are normally permanent casino employees.

PLAYERS

Professionals. They make their living predominantly from playing poker and comprise around 5% of the players who play middle limits or higher.

Stakehorses. They are called *horses* for short. They are put in games by other players or by successful business people. Normally, these are the ones who claim to be the best players. They must be good at self-promotion. They will talk about all the money they've won for people and all the tournaments they've won. Some of them are winning players, but they can't win enough to support their lifestyles or their bad habits. Many horses could also be put in the category of professionals, since they do support themselves playing poker.

Wannabes. They talk a lot about poker. They have other sources of income or family money. During their winning streaks, they view themselves as professionals. During their losing streaks, they feel they are as good as anyone, but think they are among the unluckiest card catchers on the planet. They would have a better life if they put the time and effort they spend on gambling into a more productive vocation.

Working stiffs. Some play for entertainment and others are trying to make some extra income. Some are live ones and some are winning players who derive the bulk of their income from other means.

Catalysts. Most poker games are dependent on a few action players with whom others like to play. Usually, catalysts are big losers with a large source of money, but occasionally they are winning players who give a lot of action. Those who are losing players are also called live ones, fish, pigeons, juicy players, or crazy players.

Rounders. If you show up at a card room which you rarely frequent, you may see a rounder you saw at your normal spot just hours earlier. It seems that he has no home, or maybe he has a twin.

Railbirds. They are also called *bustouts*. They intently watch all the poker games from the sidelines. They have plenty of free advice for anyone who will listen. You shouldn't take their advice too seriously, unless they are giving you advice about how not to end up like them. They look for someone who has won to give them money, often approaching winners and saying, "You know I was rooting for you!" Sometimes this is enough to get some generous players to throw them a bone.

Deadbeats. They don't hang around the cardroom for long periods of time, because they owe too many people money. They just come in when they need to find a new victim to borrow from. They have no intention of paying back their loans.

Errand boys. They are tipped or paid for their services. Typically, they do odd jobs such as taking cars to the carwash and filling them with gas or going to the store. If asked, they will do anything from shining shoes to painting houses. They aren't looking for handouts. They may not be skilled laborers, but are willing to do any job. Unfortunately, the money they make often evaporates quickly in the casino, and then they are back looking for another errand to run.

A NOTE ABOUT LIVE ONES

This somewhat derogatory term is used to describe players who lose a lot of money in games that are built around them. They are usually intelligent people who have spent their time acquiring other skills. For example, when I walk into a clothing store, an electronics supplier, or an automobile dealership, I am a live one. I'm a dream customer for a sales-

The Poker Society

man who works on commission. I make my purchases quickly and don't haggle to get the best price. Also, I have been a live one in poker games when I played at stakes too small for me to give my best effort, or when I have played badly because I was losing.

Some wealthy businessmen play poker for entertainment and competition instead of for profit. The ones I play with in high-stakes games are usually good players when they're winning, but don't handle losing as well as professional players do. When I am losing $100,000 in the game, I hope to win back $50,000 because the reduced loss is very significant to me. But to them the difference between losing $50,000 and losing $100,000 is not that great, since they don't need the money. They are more concerned about avoiding a losing session. When they are losing $100,000 their play deteriorates and they take foolish chances while trying to get even.

One businessman I know called the high-limit host at a cardroom and asked him to arrange a game. The host called back to say he had scheduled a great game with several weak players and that the businessman would be one of the better players. "I don't want to play in that game," replied the businessman. "See if you can get some better players. I want a chance to beat the best players in the world."

OTHERS

Salesmen. Some sell items like jewelry or children's toys. Others sell stolen products. Some are pushing legitimate investments, and others are scam artists. Once you become involved with salesmen, you will probably be inundated with future solicitations.

Media. The written media legitimized the poker profession with magazines and tournament reports. Television coverage has taken poker into the "sports and entertainment" business.

Loan sharks. Commonly called *juice men.* Juice men lend out money, with interest normally due on a weekly basis. The typical rate is 2% per week, but rates as high as 10% per week are not unusual. A credit card machine in a casino can be thought of as an automated juice man, since the service fees are exorbitant.

Bookies. Normally, the people who book sports bets in a casino are actually *runners* or agents for a bigger operation. They provide a service that gamblers want, and the level of their integrity can usually be verified by checking with other players.

Thieves. Thieves are rare, but an encounter with one can be disastrous. Some are card cheats who mark cards, stack the deck in deal-your-own games, or collude with partners. They may be infrequent players who think up schemes to acquire money from players in the cardroom. They might even try to take money from an unprotected dealer tray or a stack of a player's chips. Some are capable of following a player home to rob him if they think he has a lot of cash.

INSENSITIVITY OF SOME GAMBLERS

Poker players and gamblers for the most part are a callous group. Their insatiable desire to win, coupled with satisfaction from seeing their opponents lose, feeds their egocentric personalities. Here are a few real-life quotes that show how insensitive they can be.

1. When the Challenger space shuttle exploded with the first civilian observer on board, horrifying the rest of the world, legendary player Johnny Moss coldly said, "Reckon there'll be any sweaters a goin' on the next flight?" (*Sweaters* is the word for people watching a poker game.)

2. When Johnny Moss was losing in a game, the wife of a player who had just died called him and asked if he would contribute to the funeral. He said, "I'm losing my money to live people. I don't have any for the dead."

3. Jack Straus, a famous high-stakes player, received a call at the Horse-shoe Casino from a friend who was on death row. The friend said, "It looks like I will be executed. The governor didn't grant me a pardon." Jack responded, "That's pretty bad, but you won't believe what they've been doing to me here."

4. In games in different areas, players have died while playing poker, only to have someone at the table ask, "Does he have a dead hand?" In some games, a ruling has been made to declare the dead man all-in. In at least one case, in Dayton, Ohio, the dead man won the hand.

5. A group of players had just left the Mayfair Club in New York and were crossing a street in Manhattan. An elderly lady approached the club's nastiest player and asked, "Son, could you give me the time?" The player responded, "Lady, I don't give nothin' away free."

6. An abusive player collapsed at the table, a victim of an apparent heart attack. He was moved away from the table and paramedics were called, but none of the players offered assistance and the game continued. A week later the abusive player was back playing and arguing with everybody. One of the other players, Sam Perleman, apologized to the table. He said, "It's all my fault." Someone asked, "Sam, are you the one who saved him?" "No," Sam replied, "But I was right there when the paramedics were reviving him and I didn't pull them off."

7. When arguments or fights occur between players, the main interest of the others is how it will affect the game. When two volatile players are involved in a big pot, the sentiment is usually, as poker champion and gaming executive Bobby Baldwin put it, "I don't care what happens as long as someone gets hurt badly."

8. Legendary player Puggy Pearson asked his notoriously sarcastic girl-friend Cheryl Davis if she would still love him if he was broke. She said, "Of course I'd still love you Pug, and I'd miss you too."

CHAPTER 3

HOW TO BEHAVE IN THE POKER SOCIETY

"When you have to kill a man, it costs nothing to be polite."

Sir Winston Churchill
(1874-1965),
English statesman

Ace on the River

THE POKER SOCIETY HAS ITS OWN SET OF RULES AND CUSTOMS.

One of the best places to expose a person's true character is at a poker table. Many players who act appropriately in most social situations behave badly when they are losing. Some verbally abuse the dealers when they lose. They are implying that the dealers have control over the outcomes of the hands. If they believe dealers have that kind of control, you would think they would treat the dealers better in order to receive better cards. Maybe we don't really see a person's true character at the poker table, but rather, we see him at his worst.

I have come to expect to play with some people who are not very like-able. Most of them are not my friends, so I don't get upset if they don't act in a civil fashion. It comforts me that I am taking money from flawed people rather than from nice people. Players who are crybabies deserve something to cry about. A successful poker player looks for any flaw in his opponents' personalities and uses it as motivation to beat them out of their money. Fortunately, it is easy to find flaws. I like to beat up on the bad winners, bad losers, slowrollers, dealer-abusers, chauvinists, racists, ego-maniacs, lesson-givers, coffee-housers, loudmouths, etc. The only nice people I want to beat are rich people who will not suffer financially. Poker is entertainment for them, and my poker wins are only a byproduct.

Women who enter this male-dominated society will have to withstand vulgar language, sexual innuendos, and suggestions that they belong in

the kitchen rather than in the cardroom. These insults can provide them with ample motivation to win. Women also have advantages that men don't have. When women are vulnerable, male opponents will tend not to go for the kill. Additionally, a woman player will get extra action from men who are trying to prove that a woman can't beat them. The chauvinistic males in the poker society can't handle a woman outplaying them. Yet, on the river, women will get called less frequently because men don't give them credit for being able to bluff as often as men.

It is important to remember to be quiet if you are winning so you won't irritate those who are losing. The player who wins the pot should let his opponent win the argument. If you have a joke to tell, don't tell it until you are losing and the live ones are winning. I used to play in a game where we found a way to handle the problem of incessant rambling by the winning players. We made it a rule that only losers could talk. It was a very quiet game and was good training for my poker career.

Losers will not get sympathy in a poker room. Since the majority of players lose, they often enjoy and even celebrate the misery of others. It is amazing how many players, looking for sympathy, will show their losing hands and even explain how they made the right laydown, and in so doing, give away their strategy. Apparently, it is important for each of them to attract endorsements from others in his quest to be known as the unluckiest player in poker history. Of course, most of these complainers have a very selective memory. When they win a hand that they shouldn't have been in, they quickly forget, but when they get beat, they act as if they've been assaulted.

When opponents play terribly and chase me down with only a remote chance of winning, and they draw out, I don't give lessons or try to embarrass them. I remind myself about the money they have thrown away with similar plays in other pots which I have won. Every terrible starting hand and every poorly-bet hand that gets shown down assures me that I am in a good game.

Winning players sometimes have to abide by different rules than losing players. Even in retaliation, a winning player should avoid killing opponents' hands on technicalities, or needling, slowrolling, or otherwise humiliating a losing player.

I rarely show my hand when there is no showdown, even if I have made a nice bluff. An opponent who shows all his bluffs is teaching me how to beat him. I get a line on his play and can be confident I made the right play when I fold and he doesn't show his hand.

Because I often win, I try to keep a low profile so that I am perceived as just another player who suffers the ups and downs that all poker players must endure. Of course, I have had bad streaks and suffered losses, so I understand and can commiserate with players who have been losing. However, I don't give them the irrational hope that they can be as successful a gambler as I have been.

If I stay off other players' radar screens, I can fool them more often. I don't want to have my style discussed by other players. If I give the impression that I have been doing well, it only invites borrowing and staking requests, business propositions, or setups by scam artists.

I try to condition myself to be humble. If an opponent criticizes a play I made that worked out well, I don't defend myself. Without being facetious, I might say, "Stick around. I'll make worse plays than that one." If someone praises me, I remind myself that I have been fortunate. If I brag about how smart I am, how cleverly I played a hand, or how well I have been doing, in the back of my mind I say, "You deserve to lose for being so cocky." Overconfidence can lead to carelessness in decision-making. The poker gods can provide a run of bad cards that will make anyone look foolish.

In the poker society, I try to be polite to people I don't like. If I want to fight with someone, I do it over the poker table by beating him out of his money. Some people are miserable and it's miserable to be around them. Others may be desperate. I don't want to antagonize people who could make me the target of their desperation.

I don't usually socialize with my opponents. When I become too friendly with losing players or players with negative-expectation lifestyles,

How to Behave in the Poker Society

I find it uncomfortable to play hard against them and turn down their requests for money. If I am good friends with another strong winning player, losers in the game will suspect collusion and may avoid playing in games that we are both in.

It is important to prevent the catalysts in a game from destroying themselves. It's bad business to destroy people. I want the catalysts to do well enough to keep the good game surrounding them going for years. Players often talk about "killer instinct" and think all winners have to be heartless. It isn't true and isn't pragmatic.

I want the losers to feel comfortable. A winning player readily offers condolences to the unlucky card catchers around him.

Example: There was a bookie who made a lot of money booking the sports bets of high-stakes players. After a golf outing, the players played some Chinese poker and the bookie joined the game, even though he was a novice. He misplayed almost every hand and was losing badly when he said, "I never get any straights or flushes." He put down his hand with Aces in the back, Kings in the middle, and Jack-Seven-Six in the front. But he had a Jack, a Seven, and a Six for kickers in the back two hands! Everyone was silent when they saw how badly he had misplayed his hand. They all realized that he would have beaten everybody if he had played Aces in the front hand and two pair in each of the other two hands. (This play is obvious to anyone who is proficient at Chinese poker.) The bookie sensed something was wrong and asked Doyle Brunson, "Doyle, do you see any straights or flushes?" While the others were holding their breath and biting their tongues to avoid laughing, Doyle calmly replied, "No, I sure don't," and the game went on.

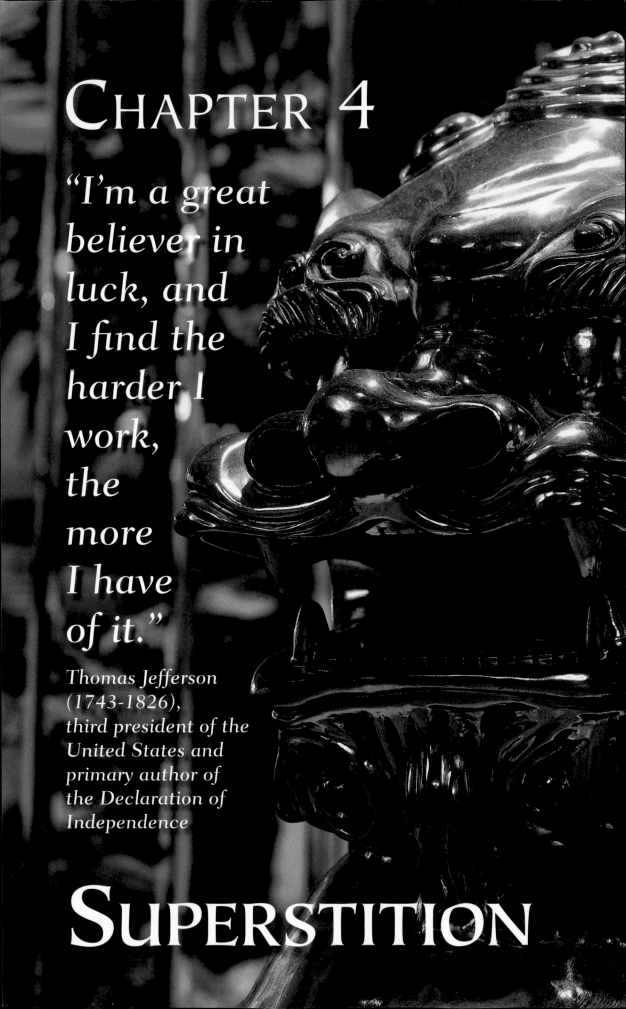

CHAPTER 4

"I'm a great believer in luck, and I find the harder I work, the more I have of it."

Thomas Jefferson (1743-1826), third president of the United States and primary author of the Declaration of Independence

SUPERSTITION

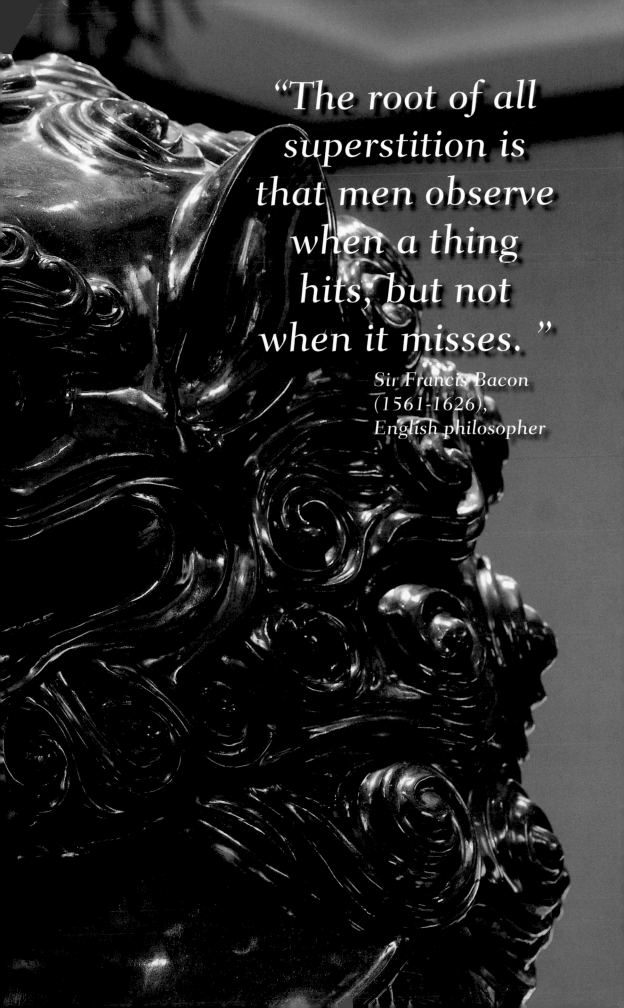

"The root of all superstition is that men observe when a thing hits, but not when it misses."

Sir Francis Bacon
(1561-1626),
English philosopher

Ace on the River

People say what fits the situation. If someone who has been winning drags another pot, a railbird will say, "He can't miss. I can't believe people are playing against him." If a big winner loses a few pots in a row, someone will comment, "He should have quit. What did he want to do, win the whole table?"

Luck is a fundamental ingredient of gambling games. It is the reason that losing players are willing to butt heads against winning players. In poker, a beginner can beat a top player on any given hand. A weak player will have winning sessions against much stronger opposition. But the poker culture so overemphasizes the role of luck that it often overlooks the importance of skill. A player who has been a steady winner for 30 years may be asked, "Are you still running good?" Players who are consistently losing are often asked, "Has your luck changed?" If people inquire about what you have done to improve your chances of winning, they are more likely to ask how you changed your luck rather than how you improved your skill.

Common superstitious tactics used by players to change their luck include scrambling the cards, changing decks, sitting out hands with an unlucky dealer, changing seating position, changing the chair they are sitting in, and even changing where their car is parked. Some players, if permitted, would change the deck after every losing hand. If they changed the deck ten times after losing ten consecutive hands, and then won the eleventh hand, they would say to themselves that they were glad they changed the deck. It would not occur to them that they might have won some of those other hands if they hadn't changed the decks.

Superstitions can lead to self-fulfilling negative prophecies. A player who believes a certain dealer has been unlucky for him in the past may play hands dealt by that dealer more tentatively. This could allow someone to draw out on him. Another player may believe that he always

Superstition

loses when his wife calls him and tells him to come home. He is probably right if it distracts him or causes him to play more hands to try to catch up quickly so he can avoid a confrontation when he gets home. Some players believe that if others comment about how much they are winning, which is called *riding the broom*, they will start to lose. Other players are afraid to make change from their lucky chips when they are winning. I see no reason to discourage my opponents from being superstitious, since anything that distracts them is probably good for me.

Streaks occur more often than some might think. One can't predict future luck from past results. Luck, whether bad or good, is a statement about the past, not the future. However, there are reasons why people who appear to be lucky continue to be lucky. First, they may just be playing better than the players who appear to be unlucky. Second, their opponents often play worse when they are losing, which only adds to the apparent good luck of those who are winning.

"What are the odds of that?" someone might ask. "One player had trip Sixes, the second had trip Sevens and the third had trip Eights all by fourth street" or "I lost with Kings nine times in a row." After something out of the ordinary happens, someone may ask what the odds are, but that is much different than if he had asked this question before he knew which peculiar thing was going to happen. This misunderstanding leads people to think something strange is going on or some freaky karma is causing this to happen.

A common saying among gamblers is, "It is unlucky to be superstitious." This is said in jest to poke fun at superstitious players, but the opposite is sometimes true. Although it may seem to contradict the first part of this chapter, your superstitions may actually be helpful if they convince you to quit when you are losing. You may not have the advantage in a game that you think you have. You may be getting cheated and not be aware that this is the reason for your bad results. If you play at two different places and usually win at one place but lose at the other, keep playing where you win, even if you think the game is better at the other place. Call it superstition if you like.

This reminds me of an anecdote about a famous mathematician:

Some colleagues visited the mathematician and saw a horseshoe over his door. When they asked him what it was for, he told them it was for good luck. "But you are a great mathematician," said one of his colleagues. "You don't believe in things like that, do you?"

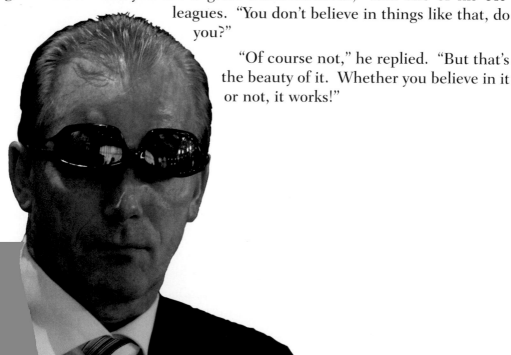

"Of course not," he replied. "But that's the beauty of it. Whether you believe in it or not, it works!"

PART II

PHILOSOPHY

CHAPTER 5

ATTITUDE OF A POKER PLAYER

"This is the business we have chosen."

Hyman Roth to Michael Corleone in The Godfather II, (1974), screenplay by Mario Puzo (1920-1999) and Francis Ford Coppola (1939-)

Ace on the River

How you handle issues in your life mirrors how you play poker.

If you read all the poker books and become a technical expert on which hands to play and how to play them, you are still likely to end up broke. You must learn how to make money and how to hold on to it.

Most people do not have the appropriate character qualities to become good poker players. Take this personality assessment test and see how you fare.

PERSONAL PROFILE QUESTIONS

1.   When a car swerves into your lane, do you yell at the other driver?

2.   Do you try to win every argument?

3.   Are you a go-getter, not wasting any time?

4.   While playing sports or other games, do you release tension by banging your fist, throwing equipment, or shouting?

5.   Do you only gamble with the odds in your favor?

6.   Are you always willing to give money to a friend so he can get into a game when he is broke?

7.   Do you accept all challenges that come your way?

8.   Do you know the value of a dollar?

9.   Do you work on the "due theory," that is, the theory that you want to play now because you have been losing and are due for a win?

10.   Are you reliable enough to arrive at the agreed-upon time to a scheduled poker game, even if you are very tired?

11.   Do you make sure you are properly funded for any game you sit down in?

12.   Do you find that drugs or alcohol loosen you up a little and help you play better?

Attitude of a Poker Player

If you answered **yes** to any of these questions, you may need some adjustments if you intend to become a professional poker player.

1. Incidents such as a car cutting you off should be handled as if they were obstacles in a video game. Just maneuver and avoid them. Dealer errors, bad rulings, and others' bad plays may cause you to lose pots. You will have to keep your composure and play on.

2. You should try to win money and let the losers win the arguments. If someone questions why you played a certain hand or attacks the way you played it, you shouldn't care. People who have weak egos try to win all the arguments they get into. A confident person doesn't need to prove he is right, especially to his opponents. If you always try to win arguments with your friends or loved ones, you should ask yourself why you need to prove you are smarter than they are. If you do it for competitive reasons, you should channel your competitiveness into more useful situations.

3. You should rest your brain before playing poker. Take care of issues that are cluttering your mind. Take steps to simplify your life. If you do a lot of intense brainwork before you play poker, you will probably wear yourself out. If you operate with many things on your mind, you are going to play on autopilot and not be aware of all the information your opponents are giving you.

Attitude of a Poker Player

4. Throwing clubs, slamming the ball to the ground, or shouting in disgust are inefficient uses of energy. An effective competitor spends time thinking about adjustments. Some famous sports figures who competed effectively and efficiently were Jack Nicklaus, Michael Jordan, Joe Montana, and Joe DiMaggio.

5. If your dealings with people are always one-sided in your favor, they may be hesitant to do business with you. People will enjoy playing with you if you give them some loose action in isolated spots. If someone suggests making a small bet on a sporting event that is being shown where you play poker, you should be willing to flip a coin to determine which side you get, but you shouldn't give action where you don't get action.

6. You shouldn't lend money to someone who you don't believe would return the favor if you needed a loan. Also, if you keep a losing player in action, you may become codependent on his or her gambling problem. There are many players walking around poker rooms who talk about what good financial shape they would be in if the people who owed them money would pay them back.

7. You don't need to fight every battle. Don't be afraid to back down if you don't like the lineup in a game. You should pass up a situation with a small advantage if you can find one with a larger advantage. You don't need to prove you are the best. To make money, you just need to find some people who play worse than you do.

8. Knowing the value of money is negatively correlated to being a good poker player. I have never heard anyone say, "He is not afraid to bluff for his last dollar, but he is a careful shopper."

9. If you continue to lose, you should find an easier game, or you may need to alter the way you are playing. If you can't find an easier game, you might take some time off to get your head straightened out. You shouldn't think you are due for a win because it is your turn to be lucky.

10. If you are tired, go back to sleep and don't show up until you are rested. If you are a player in a game with an agreed-upon starting time, you should get on a sleep schedule that allows you to show up on time, rested and ready to play. If you are too tired to play well, call and inform the host that you cannot make it, if that is an appropriate thing to do. If a late arrival is not frowned upon, as in a casino, you may arrive when only the losers are still playing, and you will have easy pickings. Also, if the game goes overnight, you will still be sharp when others are tired.

11. If a game is extremely good, get in it if you have a buy-in. There is nothing wrong with putting yourself in situations where you can win a lot more than you can lose. Don't play too tight and predictably because you are on short money. Play your game. You might go broke quickly, but if you double up, you may be on your way to a big win.

12. Although some players may play better after drinking a small amount of alcohol or using drugs, it generally gets out of hand, especially when they are losing.

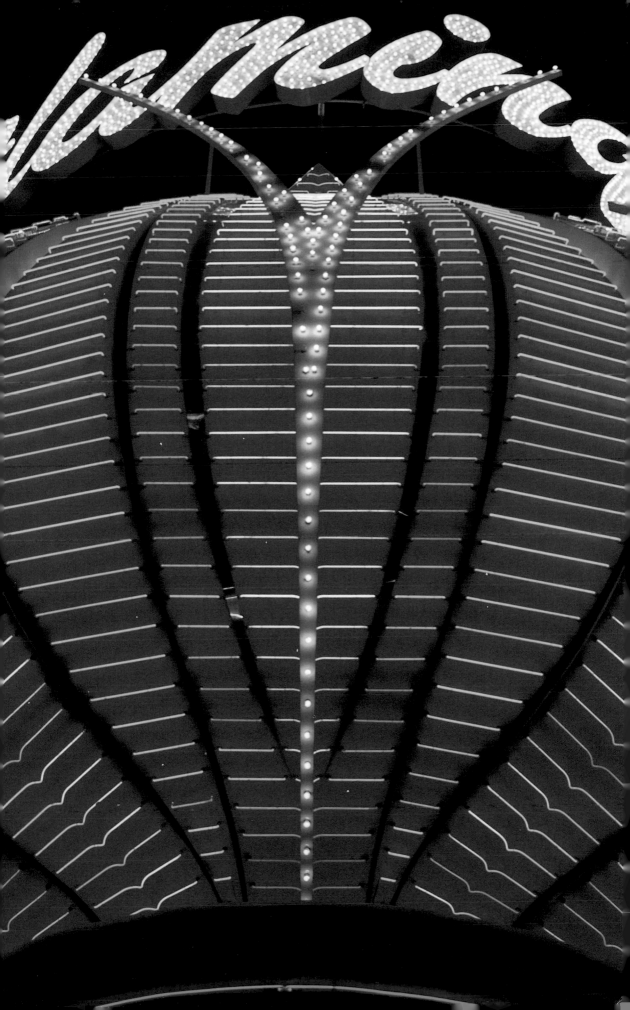

CHAPTER 6

TRAITS OF WINNING POKER PLAYERS

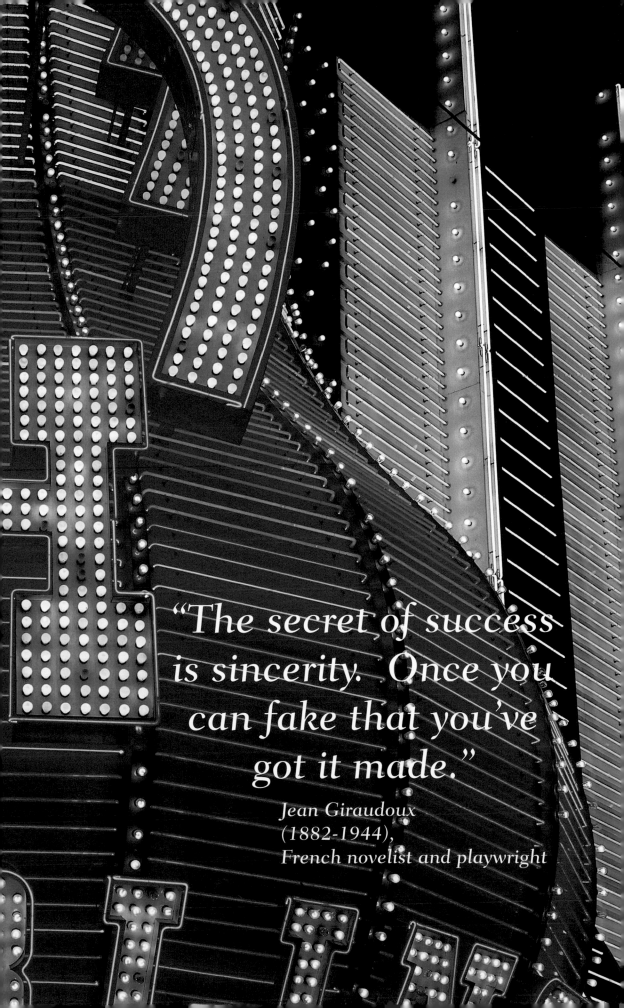

"The secret of success is sincerity. Once you can fake that you've got it made."

Jean Giraudoux
(1882-1944),
French novelist and playwright

Ace on the River

What character qualities separate winners from losers?

Pretend that we surveyed players from all the organized poker games around the world and asked them to fill in the blank: "Winning poker players are _____." If we polled the losing players, they might answer "luckier than I am." The top winners would probably have a different answer. The results of this fictitious survey are listed in reverse order.

25. **The ones with a good sense of humor.** Winning players have learned to tolerate the bad beats that happen. A gallows' sense of humor may help them endure the bad times. Of course, losing players may have lost their sense of humor over the course of time. While the winners tell jokes, the losers are saying, "Shut up and deal."

24. **Prideful.** When a winning player recognizes he is off his game, he toughens up or quits rather than give his opponents the satisfaction

of having an easy time. This can happen after an all-night session when the morning crew of rested players comes into the game. When he is losing, a winning player realizes that he is in a bad situation and goes home. Also, winning players have enough pride to avoid blaming others for their losses.

23. **Generous.** Winning players are usually big tippers. They don't place a high value on money because it comes so easily at times that it doesn't hurt to give it away. They are respectful of people who work hard for their money since, when they are running good, they don't feel they had to work very hard for it.

22. **Outgoing.** Although not essential in all gambling settings, the top players must be able to talk their way into good situations and should be gracious to losing players. There are times when they have to be able to speak up for their own best interest. Being able to talk is a plus, as long as you also know when to be quiet.

21. **Insensitive.** Good players can be cold and calculating. The only interest they have in listening to bad beat stories is the somewhat sadistic enjoyment of their opponents' misery.

20. **Optimistic.** If winners didn't believe good things were around the corner, it would be harder for them to handle some of the low points.

19. **Independent.** Winning players don't take anyone's advice without thinking about it first. Plenty of bad advice is readily available. They don't submit to peer pressure that will lead them down the bumpy path the majority has followed.

18. **Manipulative.** Winning players let others talk them into playing games or stakes that they wanted in the first place. If a seat opens to their left, and they want position on an action player, they move to the left and subtly suggest that the action player try his luck in the seat to their right.

17. **Greedy.** If a game is far more lucrative than usual, a good player will not quit, especially if he is winning. He looks at this as an opportunity to make enough money so he won't have to work as long on occasions when the game is not as juicy. In these situations, he will drive himself to stay awake for long periods. If this is too hard for you to do, perhaps you should eat healthier and exercise so you can get in better physical shape.

16. **Persistent.** Even if a good player's results have been bad, he will continue to make decisions that he believes are right.

15. **Self-centered.** Winning players understand they are in this for the money, not to please others. They don't do something that is disadvantageous for them just to be agreeable. However, they try to be smooth enough so they don't rub people the wrong way.

14. **Trustworthy.** Your word is your bond. If a player is not trustworthy, people will not want to gamble with him for fear that he will take cheap shots or bend the rules to suit his position.

13. **Aggressive.** Solid aggressive play is a trademark of a good player. An aggressive player makes his opponents pay to stay in and tries to knock out players who might otherwise win the pot. This aggressiveness is very noticeable in good female players, because men usually expect them to be passive to fit traditional stereotypes.

12. **Competitive.** A winning player is in competition to win the most money. In no-limit, he feels he can win every chip on the table.

11. **Survivors.** Many winning players are very scrappy. Some were refugees from other countries. They know life isn't always fair, and they are used to

fighting to survive. They expect obstacles and believe they can overcome them. In the Darwinian sense, winning players are survivors of the poker battle.

10. **Empathetic.** A good player understands how other people feel and what they are thinking. He can often figure out the conclusion

another player will come to before it happens.

9. **Fearless.** Winning players aren't afraid to pull the trigger. That is, they aren't afraid to make the right play, even if it is risky. But they are careful not to go too far and become reckless. Recklessness, when it works, can be mistaken for bravery.

8. **Able to think under pressure.** When a good player is losing, he is still able to take the right action. Many people shut their brains off and stop thinking when the pressure is on. They don't want to face how badly they are playing. Some players use alcohol to impede their thought processes.

7. **Attentive to detail.** A winning player may describe a hand like this: "Seat number four raised in early position after having lost two pots in a row. I called on the button with Ace-Jack offsuit and the big blind was the only other caller. The flop came 10-8-3 with two hearts. After the big blind checked, seat four hesitated slightly as he bet and I decided to raise him, since I had the Ace of hearts and I didn't think he had anything." When a weak player tells the same story, he often forgets

how many players were in the pot, who raised, and who had the Ace of hearts. He doesn't note any hesitation or the psychological state of his opponent.

Traits of Winning Poker Players

6. **Motivated.** You may need to convince yourself that you must win. It is easy to get lazy when you have no immediate money pressure. There are players who splash around in side games, but play tournaments very well. They are more motivated by glory than money. Some high-stakes players don't take tournaments very seriously because, if they get knocked out, they can make more money in the side games.

5. **The ones with the best memories.** Winning players have a memorized basic strategy. They also remember what worked and what didn't. They have a mental catalogue of every opponent's playing style and idiosyncrasies.

4. **In control of their emotions.** Although some players try to talk their opponents into making wrong decisions, most winning players are quiet during each hand and maintain the proverbial poker face. Even after losing a hand, they don't show their disappointment. They don't let their opponents get into their heads.

3. **Intelligent.** Winning players are able to formulate strategies and alter them when they are not working. Intelligence is the ability to adapt to one's environment. The most important part of the poker environment is the opponents in the game. An intelligent player is able to deduce what his opponents are doing, what they are likely to do, and how to use this information to his maximum advantage.

2. **Honest with themselves.** Winning players admit to themselves when they are playing badly. They take a break and refocus. If they are being outplayed, they are able to objectively judge whether the game is worth sitting in.

1. **Psychologically tough.** The best don't give in, no matter how severe the psychological beating. Most players tend to blame losses on outside circumstances: "Of course I lost. I always lose after I argue with my girlfriend," or "Whenever I make one bad decision, I know I'm going to take some bad beats." Psychologically tough players have

the mindset that they can win in any situation and can overcome anything. You cannot judge a player until you see how he handles adversity. This is where the top players differentiate themselves.

Some people, when referring to someone they think is a great player, may point out that he is lacking in a number of the traits mentioned above. Maybe that player isn't as successful as he appears to be. He could probably do much better if he improved in those areas where he is deficient.

A few of the above characteristics are considered negative personality traits. A good player should recognize this and try to improve his behavior in interpersonal relationships away from the poker table.

Here are some characteristics good players may not have:

Athletic. Many of the better players were good athletes when they were young because their competitiveness was channeled into sports. Some try to stay in good shape, but the sedentary lifestyle will take its toll on most of them.

From a wealthy family. Coming from an affluent environment is a big detriment. Spoiled rich kids are not likely to be tough enough to become top players.

Compassionate. Compassion is a combination of empathy and sympathy. A good player has the first, but not much of the second. He expects no sympathy, and any that he gives is usually patronizing.

Educated. Being educated is often a result of circumstance. This includes where a person grew up, the extent to which education was stressed, how much supervision there was, and how motivated the person was to learn. Many people from third world countries or lower socioeconomic situations are intelligent, but didn't have the opportunity to become well educated. Conversely, most highly educated people have jobs that don't allow them to spend much time playing poker.

Overconfident. Overconfidence will hamper a player's ability to accurately evaluate his edge in gambling situations.

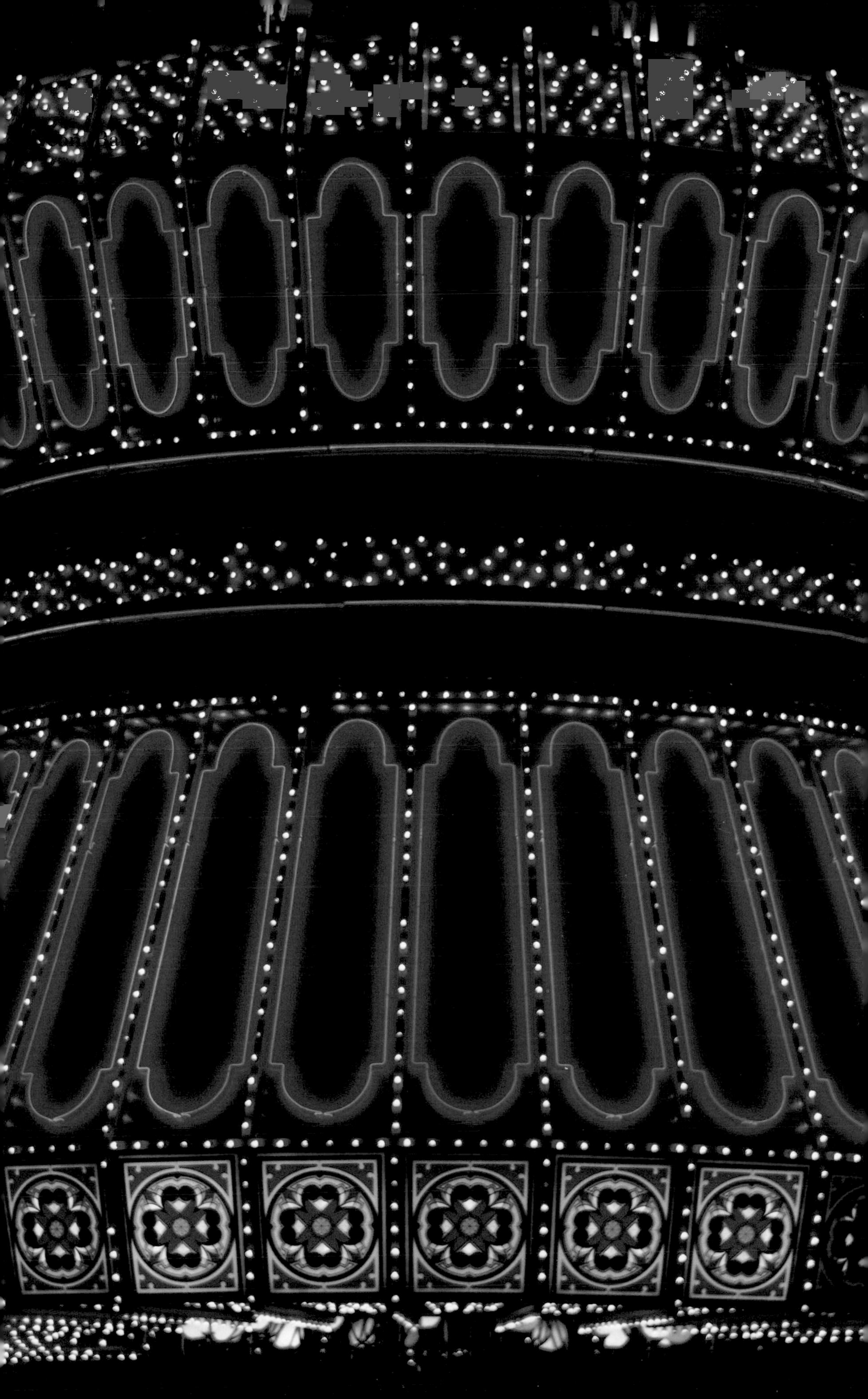

CHAPTER 7

PSYCHOLOGY OF GAMBLING

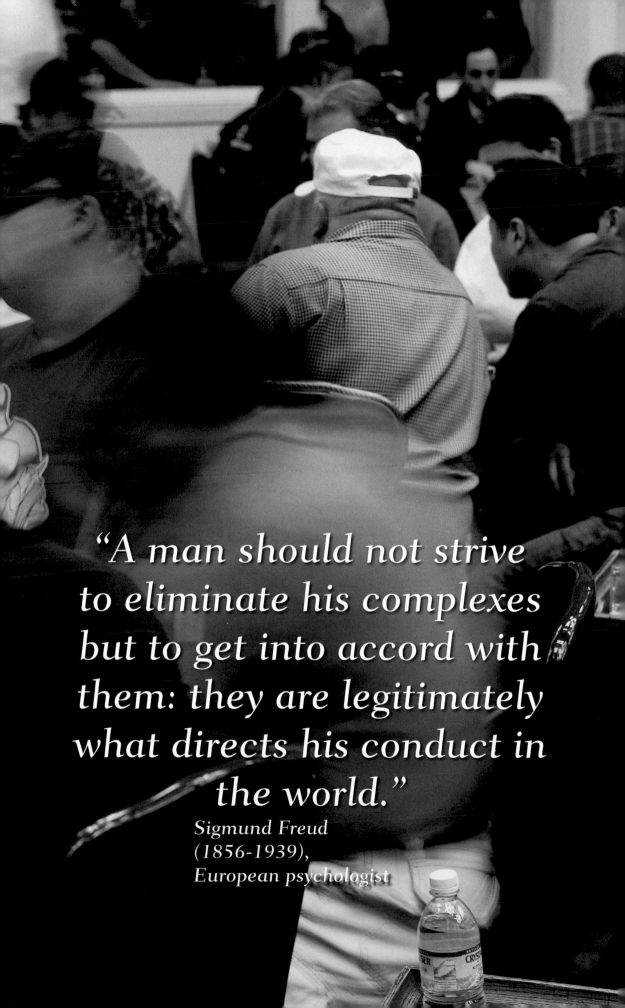

"A man should not strive to eliminate his complexes but to get into accord with them: they are legitimately what directs his conduct in the world."

Sigmund Freud (1856-1939), European psychologist

Ace on the River

**POKER IS MORE THAN A GAME WHERE ONE SET
OF CARDS IS COMPARED TO ANOTHER WITH
THE BETTER HAND WINNING. IT IS A GAME
OF PERSONALITIES. UNLESS YOU KNOW YOURSELF
BETTER THAN ANYONE ELSE DOES, YOU WILL
BE AT A DISADVANTAGE.**

Gamblers tend to be competitive people with compulsive tendencies. It is helpful to have some knowledge of extreme behavior, so you can stop yourself when you start down a path that is self-destructive.

THE COMPULSIVE GAMBLER INSIDE OF YOU

To be successful, you have to come to terms with the compulsive gambler inside of you. Successful gamblers are compulsive winners. They know how to exploit an advantage, but if they were less intelligent or less skilled, they might have ended up in Gamblers Anonymous.

TYPES OF COMPULSIVE GAMBLERS:

1. **Thrill seeker.** Wants the adrenaline rush. This type is also likely to get involved with drugs.

2. **Depressive.** Gambles to forget problems or as a diversion from depression. This type is also likely to use alcohol to avoid facing problems.

3. **Approval seeker.** Needs to be validated. Wants to prove how smart he is. Being on the right side is important, so he can justify to himself and others that he knows what he is doing.

4. **Outcast.** Needs to be around other people and is willing to gamble and lose to be part of the gambling environment.

5. **Fatalist.** Feels he has no control over his fate. Thinks some people are lucky and some are unlucky. Gambles to find out what his future will hold. This kind of philosophy is well-accepted in some cultures.

6. **Short-term planner.** Looks for loopholes and the easy way to success. He is afraid to miss out on a winning situation. Every event he could have bet on, but didn't, becomes a missed opportunity.

7. **Desperado.** Needs money now. Willing to take any risk. Feels every situation is his last shot.

8. **Conditioned gambler.** Anyone could fall into this category. For most of us, winning is fun and rewarding, while losing is unenjoyable and distressing. When a novice gambles for the first time and loses, people often think that it may be the best for him in the long run. This dose of reality may prevent him from thinking gambling is easy money. If the novice has early success, this positive reinforcement may condition him to expect success from gambling, leading to harder times when the inevitable losses come.

Consider these experiments with laboratory mice. Mice are put in a cage with a button that they can push with their paws. The button is connected so that the experimenter has the option of allowing the button to give the mouse an electric shock or give the mouse a food pellet from a chute next to the button.

Mouse #1 is given a shock the first time he presses the button. He spends most of his time away from the area where the button is. If the button ever gets pressed again, it will be accidental. Mouse #1 has been conditioned to associate pressing the button with getting an electric shock.

Mouse #2 gets a food pellet when he presses the button. He presses the button often and seems to enjoy his environment. But after many presses, Mouse #2 is given a shock. He waits a little while and tries again. If given another shock, Mouse #2 will stay away from the button. He believes, and rightly so, that something has changed the function of the button. If he gets hungry enough, he may try the button again. Mouse #2 was originally conditioned to associate the button press with receipt of a food pellet, but now that conditioning has been extinguished.

Now the most interesting case: occasionally feeding and shocking Mouse #3. First we give Mouse #3 a food pellet, then a shock, then a couple of food pellets, then a few shocks. Mouse #3 realizes that sometimes he will get food pellets and sometimes shocks, but he cannot predict what is coming. Once we have him conditioned in this fashion, we stop giving him food pellets and only give him shocks. Mouse #3 has learned that eventually he will get a food pellet if he presses enough times. What do you think he will do if we never give him a food pellet? The answer: He will shock himself to death. This experiment shows that intermittent reinforcement is the hardest kind to extinguish.

Now make this analogy from mice to humans: think of a food pellet as a winning gambling session and an electric shock as a losing session. People who win enough times to keep their hopes up are able to withstand the shock of losing. This intermittent reinforcement may cause people to keep gambling until they have lost everything: their businesses, their families, and in some cases their lives.

Know your weaknesses better than anyone else. Don't be afraid to admit them to yourself. Suppose you enjoy betting on sports, but you increase your bets when you lose as you try to get even. You have a problem that may only be solved by promising yourself never to bet on sports again.

Psychology of Gambling

To a gambler, money is worthless and all-important at the same time. Money is just chips for playing and keeping score. In the gambling world, everything is evaluated in terms of money. "How much would you take to cut off your arm?" "How much would you pay to get that girl?" "Why would

you go scuba diving? You can't make money doing that." Casino personnel will greet you with, "Good to see you, Mr. G," when you have money, but tell you, "Please back away from the table," when you are hanging around broke.

PATTERNS OF MEN IN CASINOS

Some potential dangers are sports betting, strip clubs, loan sharks, codependency on losers, alcohol, and drugs.

PATTERNS OF WOMEN IN CASINOS

Relatively few women are successful poker players. They typically started playing poker later in life than men because of the stigma attached to gambling. Some were not encouraged to be competitive when they were young. They may have avoided seedy environments or felt unwelcome in the gambling environment. Losing can lead to lower self-esteem, which causes some women to use themselves as a marketable commodity.

CHAPTER 8

BRAIN CHEMISTRY

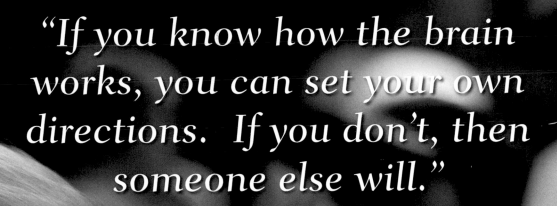

"If you know how the brain works, you can set your own directions. If you don't, then someone else will."

Richard Bandler
(1950-),
American therapist

Ace on the River

POKER PLAYERS TEND TO BE BORDERLINE COMPULSIVE. TAKE CARE OF YOUR BRAIN OR YOU MAY GO OVER THE EDGE.

Grammar school biology view of the brain: The brain is the controlling organ of the central nervous system, which acts like a mass of electrical wires sending impulses that control all of the functions in the body.

High school biology view of the brain: The brain, the spinal cord, and the rest of the nervous system are made up of nerve cells which are called neurons. Most of the neurons are covered with a coating called myelin to prevent short-circuiting. Myelin gives the brain its whitish color. Neurons can become stimulated, which causes a small electrical impulse. This impulse is transmitted along a branch-like appendage of the neuron, called the axon. The impulse is received in an adjacent neuron at a tentacle-like location, called the dendrite. The gap between the axon of one neuron and the dendrite of another is called the synapse. Eventually, the impulse reaches an appropriate neuron next to a muscle or gland, which produces a response.

Brain Chemistry

College biochemistry view of the brain: Using an electron microscope and chemical staining techniques, we can detect that the electrical impulses in the brain are transmitted at the synapses using chemicals. The electrical charge in a neuron stimulates the axon to release a chemical, called a neurotransmitter, and sends it to the receiving cell across the synapse. This chemical stimulates the receiving cell, causing it to have an electrical charge, and then the process is repeated.

There are several neurotransmitters. The main ones are noradrenaline, dopamine, serotonin, and GABA. Studies have shown correlations between psychological problems and levels of certain neurotransmitters at the nerve synapses in the brain. The neurotransmitter that is most relevant to gambling is serotonin. Studies have shown that people with compulsive disorders have less serotonin at the synapses in the brain than people who are not deemed to be compulsive. In the future, studies may show other physiological and environmental factors correlated to compulsion, but currently the serotonin-compulsion connection is the best understood.

Prescription drugs, such as Prozac®, Zoloft®, Luvox®, and Paxil®, are commonly used to increase serotonin levels at nerve synapses. Nutrition also has an effect on brain chemistry. Most gamblers may not need medication, but as a group their serotonin levels are lower than normal. If you put Prozac® in the bottled water at your local casino, you would diminish the compulsion to gamble to such a degree that the casino would probably have to shut down.

On the other hand, recreational drug use may cause nerve damage and alter brain chemistry, which will induce symptoms of psychological disorders such as anxiety, fatigue, depression, bipolar behavior, compulsive behavior, schizophrenic behavior, and paranoia. The chemical changes and nerve damage will also impair memory and judgment. Since gamblers tend to be compulsive, they are more likely than the general population to get hooked on drugs or alcohol. To make matters worse, once they are hooked, the effects will be more pronounced if their brain chemistry was barely normal to start with.

CHAPTER 9

INTEGRITY

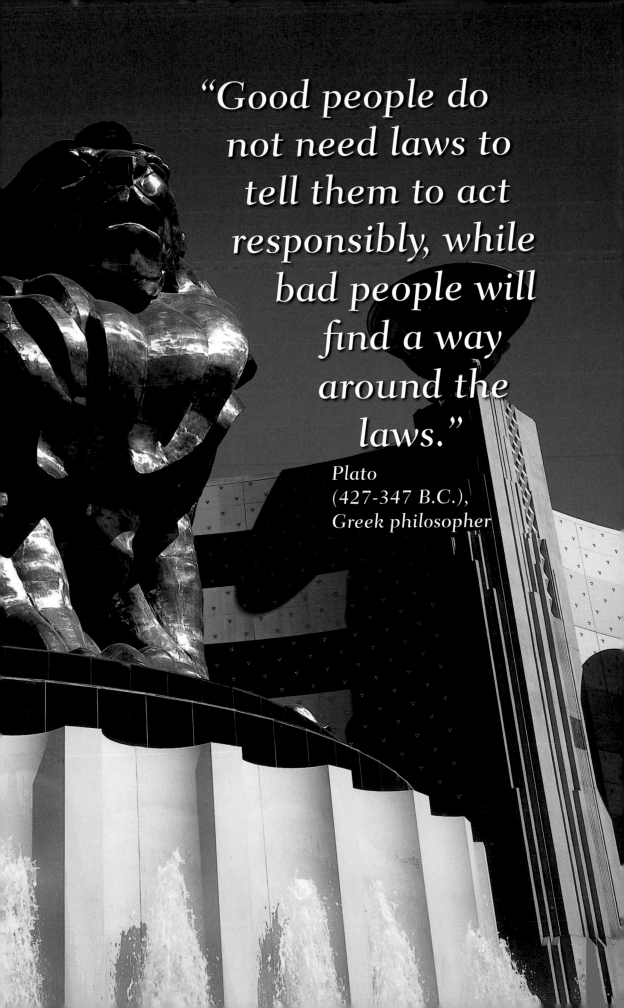

"Good people do not need laws to tell them to act responsibly, while bad people will find a way around the laws."

Plato
(427-347 B.C.),
Greek philosopher

Ace on the River

**I FOLLOW A STRICTER SET OF ETHICAL
GUIDELINES THAN MOST OF MY OPPONENTS,
EVEN IF IT COSTS ME MONEY IN THE SHORT RUN.
IT HAS GIVEN ME INNER PEACE, AND IN THE
LONG RUN I HAVE ACTUALLY
PROFITED FROM IT.**

We all know people we would call shot-takers or angle-shooters, who enforce the rules selectively, bend the rules, or breach the etiquette of the game. Different people draw the line at different places as to when this constitutes cheating. Some examples are: hesitating to see what your left-hand opponent is going to do, pretending to bet, sneaking a peek at someone's hole cards, not mentioning that someone has put too many chips in the pot, objecting to string raises even though players routinely make them despite the rules technically forbidding them, correcting overlooked hands on a selective basis, and "victory ripping" losing hands with the hope that the winner will throw his hand away. I try to be honest even in borderline areas.

Some players believe they are justified when they disregard the rules against someone who has cheated. Others believe it is acceptable to disregard the rules against someone who *may* cheat them. Still others believe that they are above the rules and everyone is fair game. If you are scru-

Integrity

pulously honest, no one is likely to cheat you in retaliation or because he thinks you may cheat him.

Dishonesty gets in the way of a winning player. If losers are in a game with suspicious activity, they will have a reason to stop playing. Conversely, players will like to play with you as long as they know you play honestly. I try to set a standard for obeying the rules against all opponents. If I can gain the respect of the other players, they may follow my lead.

If you owe money, which will probably happen sometime, make sure no one ever has to chase you down. Be dependable. You may need to borrow from one source to pay another. If there is a time that you don't want to pay your debts because it will leave you with a short bankroll, pay the debts anyway. Your reliability in these matters will result in you having a virtual bankroll far greater than the actual money you have.

It is the responsibility of the person who owes money to mention the amount owed and his plans for making payment whenever he meets his lender. This may alleviate the hard feelings and misunderstandings that often accompany indebtedness.

CHAPTER 10

GETTING

YOUR

EDUCATION

"I think everyone should go to college and get a degree and then spend six months as a bartender and six months as a cabdriver. Then they would really be educated."

Al McGuire
(1928-2001),
American basketball coach

"Education costs money, but then so does ignorance."

Sir Moser Claus
(1922-),
German-born British
Academic

Ace on the River

MOST PLAYERS DON'T HAVE A LONG-TERM PLAN TO IMPROVE THEIR PLAYING ABILITY.

We have heard about the superstar athlete who has the choice of turning pro before finishing college. Most people feel that he should stay in school, gain some maturity, and learn how to manage money better. The exception is when his family has pressing financial problems or the risk of injury is deemed too great. Poker players should also stay in school so they will have a career to fall back on. I have seen many poker players destroyed because they lacked the maturity they might have achieved if they had stayed in college.

Getting good grades is also a game. The discipline required to be a successful gambler is greater than that needed to be a good student. The best degree for a poker player is a major in psychology with a minor in mathematics. A few business courses wouldn't hurt.

If you are an up-and-coming player, you should be an avid reader of poker literature and articles. Even if you don't agree with what is written, you will gain insight into how others think the games should be played. When you disagree, you should think about how you can exploit the weaknesses in their strategy. This will help you play against people whose strategies differ from yours.

The fact that you are reading this suggests that you read about poker and have some idea of what reasonable starting hands are in the games you play. If you see players who play garbage hands but have consistently good results, you should analyze what else they do that makes them successful. Maybe they bet their hands well. Maybe the effect of them playing a wider variety of hands confuses other players and makes those players play badly.

Getting Your Education

You cannot learn to play at a higher level without playing against better opponents. When you have mastered the game you are in, you may want to try to move up in stakes. However, avoid becoming a victim of the Peter Principle, which states that people keep moving up until they reach their level of incompetence. If you move to a

level where you are unsuccessful, move back down and think about what those players were doing better than you were.

Any time a new form of poker starts catching on in your area, try to become proficient at it as quickly as possible. You may get an advantage over your local opponents by traveling to areas that specialize in different games. You will be able to incorporate the techniques of the better players into your own strategy and use them when you get back home. Go to the eastern part of the United States for stud, the West for limit hold'em and Ace-to-Five lowball, the South for pot-limit and no-limit, Europe for pot-limit Omaha, and Las Vegas for Omaha Eight-or-better. If you frequently play with people from different areas, keep a notebook cataloging their styles, tells, and steam points.

With regard to poker players and Las Vegas, it is true that "If you can make it there, you can make it anywhere," but not necessarily for the reasons the Las Vegas players believe. Las Vegas professionals bristle at the suggestion that they are not the best at all forms of poker. I don't think they are. However, they *are* the cream of the crop at the gamesmanship, survival, and moneymaking skills that are mentioned in this book. This accounts for their success at gambling.

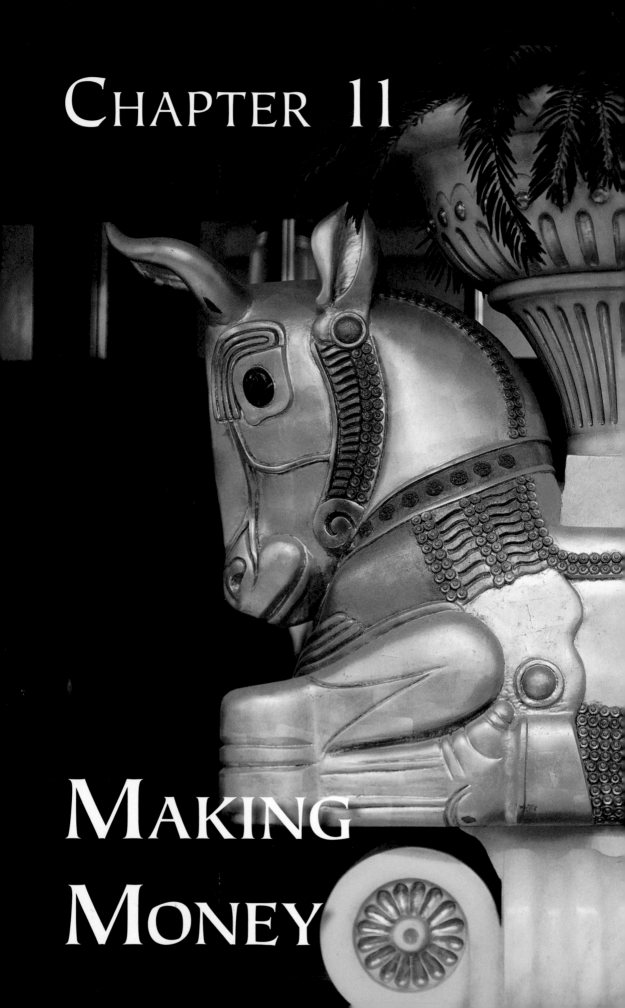

CHAPTER 11

MAKING MONEY

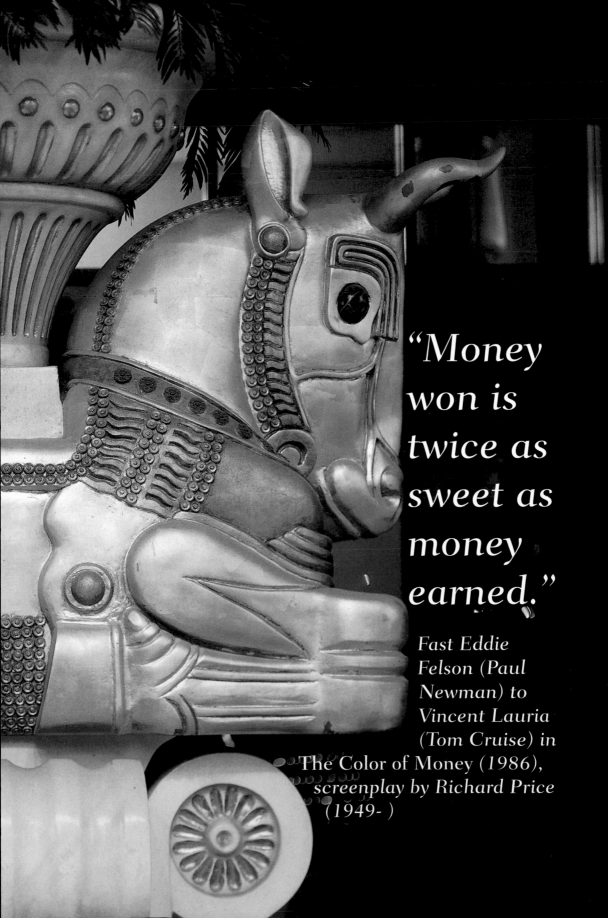

"Money won is twice as sweet as money earned."

Fast Eddie Felson (Paul Newman) to Vincent Lauria (Tom Cruise) in The Color of Money (1986), screenplay by Richard Price (1949-)

Ace on the River

Even if you know how to play poker, you still must learn how to make money.

With the increase in poker literature, poker tutorial software, and Internet poker, the gap between the play level in middle-limit games and high-limit games has been greatly reduced. Surprisingly, there are players in the middle limits who play their hands better than winning players in higher-limit games. These middle-limit players are not able to move up because they lack certain moneymaking and money handling skills. We are in an era in which players have superior technical skills compared to the players of the past, but are weaker psychologically. Part of the weakness is due to the fact that nowadays the better young players start playing tournaments and don't learn the skills necessary for survival in side action.

Let's pretend you are at a bowling alley where the bowlers regularly bet against each other. You are a 170 average bowler. One group of bowlers averages around 190 and another group averages around 150. If you want to make money, bowl with the 150 average bowlers. In bowling, they would probably not bet against you, but in poker, players of all abilities play against each other without a handicap. You may want to improve your technique so that you can bowl with the 190 average bowlers because they gamble for higher stakes, but for now stay where you can make a profit.

The bowling analogy illustrates the importance of game selection. Unfortunately, many low-limit and middle-limit players are not able to determine who the 150 average bowlers are. They use starting hands as the only means of evaluation. They see themselves as 200 average bowlers because they think they

Making Money

know what hands to start with and how to play them. After careful consideration, they may come up with the correct way to bet a hand, but that doesn't mean they will make that play in tempo, in a real game situation. They see someone win with a bad hand, but they don't notice that the player bets his hands well or pushes people around and gets them to play badly.

When I am evaluating a game, I don't waste energy comparing myself to the better players in the game. I focus on the weaker players. They are the ones I will be winning most of the money from. If there are a couple of players who play much worse than I do, it is a good game. If there is one extremely weak player, it is a good game.

In addition to selecting lucrative games with weak players, I want to get on a schedule that allows me to play when the games are typically weak. For some poker games, it is good to get there when the game starts to assure a seat with the live players. In other poker games, the action usually starts out slowly, so it is better to wait until you can play with the players who are stuck. You will learn to tell the difference based on your experience with the particular players who make up the game.

Why play when you have a slight edge, if you can wait until you have a big edge? Even if you have a slight edge, is it enough to compensate for the time (house rake) you have to pay? Fewer than 20% of poker players win enough to cover the time, fewer than 10% win enough to pay their living expenses, and fewer than 5% win enough to also offset their bad habits.

How much of an advantage can a player expect to have over his opponents? First we have to decide how much action he gets on his money. That varies according to the player's style of play and the play of his opponents. There are differences depending on which games are played and what structures are used in the games. Total action depends greatly on the speed at which the games are dealt. For the sake of discussion, we will as-

sume that a typical player in limit-poker games will get action on around 33 big bets per hour. If he shows a profit of one big bet per hour, we can say he has earned around 3% on his action, which we call a 3% advantage. A player with a 3% advantage will be a consistent winner. A typical standard deviation, for the statistically minded, is around 10 big bets per hour.

Sometimes the game is just not that good. Especially if you have been losing recently, it may be better to move down to a juicier lower-limit game, if it is available. If you don't normally act like a big shot, it will be psychologically easier for you to move down. This is an example of turning down the challenge to beat the bigger game. When I go to lower limits, I tell myself I am working.

There are a few reasons for playing in a marginally lucrative or even a bad game. If it will not greatly impact your bankroll, a mediocre game may serve as practice to sharpen your skills against tough opponents. Or possibly, the game may get better if weaker players jump in. Even if this doesn't happen, players who are normally tough may get stuck and become live ones themselves.

You should prepare yourself to play all forms of poker that are played in a casino. When mixed games are played, there are always some players who are weak at some of the games. If you are one of them, practice playing your weaker games for smaller stakes. You should become sufficiently skilled in all forms of poker so you won't have to pass up an extremely good game. When negotiating which games to play, your choices should be more dependent on your opponents' weaknesses than on your strengths. Sometimes you may vote against playing a game in which you are very proficient if it will cause your opponents to play a game in which you have a bigger relative advantage. For example, if your opponents are better at hold'em than stud, you may suggest playing half hold'em and half stud instead of straight hold'em.

Serious poker players don't want to miss out on some good games because they live too far from the place where they normally play. If you have good contacts and you live less than 30 minutes away, you will be able to get a seat in the especially good games that occasionally occur. If a floorman's phone call enables you to get a seat in a good game, make sure you tip him when you sit down.

Good games in casinos sometimes go around the clock for days or even months. Some players, when they are stuck, play more than 24 hours and are easy prey for rested players. I quit when I am tired and reenter the game after I have slept. If I am at a casino that isn't open 24 hours a day or at a home game that has a definite ending time, I will try to be there for the last hour. There will usually be losers who are playing badly because they are trying to get even. Hopefully, I won't be one of them.

If there is a bigger game around than the one you normally play in, you should always be aware of which players are the extreme live ones who occasionally frequent the game. If you have been doing okay, you should take a shot at that bigger game even if you feel you can afford just one minimum buy-in. Big wins in poker occur by being at the right place at the right time when reckless players are throwing their money away.

If I am playing in a game that seems extremely lucrative, I will play all night. I usually don't quit until two strong, rested players enter the game. If the game stays good, I will play until it breaks up or I am totally exhausted. Undisciplined players take their wins too early, deciding they have earned the right to enjoy themselves for a day or two. This takes the pressure off of their opponents and is a bad management mistake that often goes unnoticed.

Most of us start chasing too much with the worst hand when we are losing. When I am stuck and realize that I am playing badly, I will get up, go to the bathroom, wash my face, and have a good talk with myself. I give myself an ultimatum that if I continue to play badly, I will have to quit. Then I go back into the game, and if I continue to play badly, I *do* quit.

Sometimes it is possible to create a good game by changing the limit and taking players out of their comfort level. Raising the limit can make it uncomfortable for some players to make the correct aggressive plays.

Ace on the River

Lowering the limit can cause some to play too loosely because the stakes are smaller than they are accustomed to.

From past experience, you should have a reasonable idea of how much each opponent has to lose before he tends to go on tilt. This amount is called his steam point. Some players have a steam point of one buy in, while others have a steam point of a certain round amount. Some steam anytime they are losing, and some steam whenever they lose a big pot, even if they are ahead. If a player is close to his steam point, you may decide to keep playing in a game you would otherwise quit. Once he reaches his steam point, you will have to call him down much more than you normally would.

If you are serious about making money, don't put yourself in situations where you can lose a lot and win a little. Don't play only to get even, and avoid trying to win a little more to get to a round number. If someone buys in illegally short, either object, take a walk, quit, or go in with him so he can have a legitimate buy-in. With the exception of this case, you should not take on partners. It's dangerous to let other players use your money when it is a large part of your bankroll. If you are the one playing with partnership money, you may be afraid to make what you think is the right play if it is risky. You won't want to explain what happened if the play turns out badly.

The only times you should set a limit on how much you can win is when it would jeopardize the future of the game if you beat a catalyst for too much, when some of the money is on credit and you may not get paid, or when you know the live one is almost out of money.

You may decide to quit before the game breaks up because you are tired or you have other commitments. If you are winning, you should keep playing until you lose some money back. On occasion, this strategy will allow you to win much more than you had envisioned. This also has the added bonus of conditioning yourself to handle your losses better, since you will generally quit on a losing note. You should not quit at your high point unless the game breaks up, the live one quits and the game is no good, or you are playing no-limit and are afraid to be aggressive enough to gamble when necessary.

If you are a good poker player, it will seem that money *does* grow on trees. However, you should remember that when winter comes, there might be no leaves to be found. You may have lucrative games to play in now, but they won't go on forever. Games are usually very dependent on a small group of players. Make money while the making is good.

CHAPTER 12

HOLDING
ON TO
MONEY

"A fool and his money are soon parted. I would pay anyone a lot of money to explain that to me."

Homer Simpson, cartoon creation of Matt Groening (1954-)

Ace on the River

You must protect your bankroll.

All the bills are finally paid and you feel pretty good. Is it time to go shopping? Yes, providing you leave enough money to play poker. Money is the tool of your trade. A carpenter wouldn't give his tools away and you should be careful not to give yours away either. How much you need depends on what stakes you play for and how good you are relative to the games in which you play. If you have a 3% edge, you should allow for four big losses, which is about 200 big bets in limit poker. If you have less than a 1% edge, you are at risk and may need to find easier games.

You will not always have enough money with you everywhere you play. It is advisable to have a lending arrangement with a few select winning and honorable players. You can have an agreement to lend to each other with an understanding that the money will be paid the next time you play together. Don't borrow money from someone if you don't want to reciprocate the favor. Don't borrow on juice (high interest) or lend to people who do.

You will occasionally lend money to players who do not pay you back when they should. When they finally offer to pay you, don't be nice and say, "I know you owe other people. Pay them first." Don't refuse payment or partial payment that you are owed. Allowing people to pay you piecemeal helps them too. They may have difficulty holding onto enough money to pay in one installment.

I try to stay out of financial relationships with people who don't pay when they should have. All too often, soon after they pay off a debt, they borrow the money back. If you have this arrangement, you might as well not collect, since the money is really theirs. They just let you hold it occasionally. There will be other unreliable people whom you may decide to help, either out of the goodness of your heart or because you are not good at saying no. When you are in good shape, you may not care. However, it can be

Holding on to Money

very aggravating and financially debilitating when your shortage of money starts dictating which games you can play in, while many people owe you money. This may sound heartless, but sometimes you have to ask yourself, "If I didn't exist, what would happen to the people I help finance?" They would get help from someone else or would stop coming to the cardroom, which might be good for them.

Poker players are the worst investors in the world. When they have extra money, they think that making investments is a responsible way to handle their money. Because they are accustomed to generating large returns from small investments in poker, they are under the impression that the business world works the same way. If someone enthusiastically offers them a "can't miss" investment opportunity, they don't realize that the presenter has already exhausted all normal means of capitalization. Now he is scraping the bottom of the barrel looking for people with disposable cash. Professional investors think about rates of return in the 10% to 20% range, with hopes for something better. When gamblers invest, they expect to at least double their money, or even make ten times their money or more, if things go well.

STEPS THAT A WISE INVESTOR TAKES:

1. Reads the business plan or prospectus.

2. Talks to experts in the field.

3. Estimates the demand for the product.

4. Evaluates the quality of the product.

5. Assesses the competition.

6. Determines why the investment opportunity is available (i.e., why large investors or companies with similar products didn't invest in it).

7. Determines what share of the company he will get for his money.

8. Compares his share to that of other investors and employees of the company, especially the executives.

9. Calculates the expected rate of return and establishes a time frame.

10. Verifies that the proper accounting procedures are in place so he will get his fair share.

STEPS THAT A POKER PLAYER TAKES:

1. Asks how much money is needed.

2. When the money runs out, asks how much more is needed to keep the business going.

3. Repeats step 2.

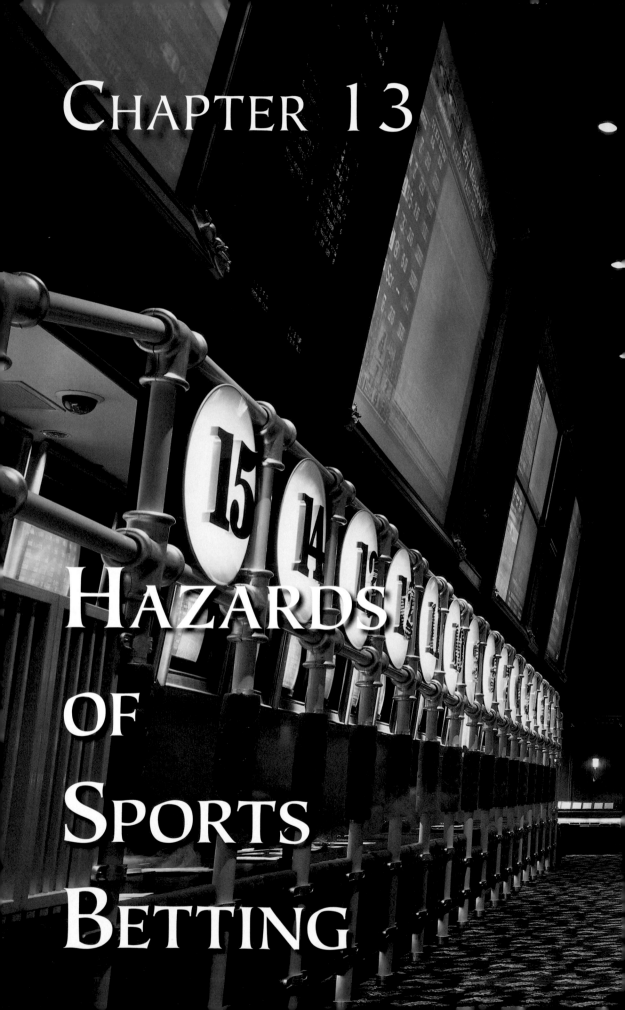

CHAPTER 13

HAZARDS OF SPORTS BETTING

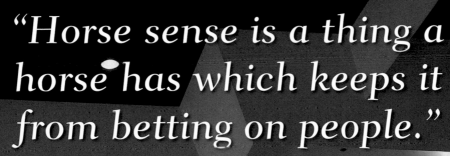

"Horse sense is a thing a horse has which keeps it from betting on people."

W. C. Fields
(1880-1946),
American actor and humorist

Ace on the River

SPORTS BETTING IS PREVALENT IN THE POKER WORLD. ALTHOUGH THIS CHAPTER DOESN'T FALL UNDER THE HEADING OF "POKER INSTRUCTION," IT CONTAINS ADVICE THAT MAY HELP PLAYERS AVOID PITFALLS THAT CAN DERAIL THEM.

Most poker players like to gamble on other games, such as gin rummy, backgammon, golf, pool, blackjack, and craps. But their most common gambling activity other than poker is sports betting because it requires less effort than the other activities. While some poker players make a substantial portion of their income in these endeavors, this discussion is intended for those who dabble at these games for action or are taking a shot to win some quick money. Unless he has a good edge in these other activities, a poker player should limit the time and money he invests in them.

Even if a player is able to make money at these other games, here are some negative aspects he should consider:

Hazards of Sports Betting

1. He is taking time away from his poker playing where he can make up to 3% on continual action, so his edge is realized over a larger amount of money.

2. He may be depriving himself of much needed rest as a result of betting on these other activities. For example, he may get up to watch a sporting event when he should be sleeping.

3. He is damaging his work ethic, since easy-money scenarios make it hard to work at poker. He may think, "Why grind it out at poker, when I can make a quick $5000 betting on a basketball game?"

Just among high-stakes poker players in California and Nevada, millions of dollars are lost each year to bookies who have runners frequenting the casinos.

Every year, in poker games around the world, the following sequence of events occurs. Some poker-playing sports bettor suggests to other players, "Why don't we save the juice and bet among ourselves?" (The *juice*, typically 10% on a losing bet, is the commission a bookie charges for giving you the choice of sides.) Most of the players agree that betting against each other when they like opposite sides is a money-saving idea. But an enterprising player decides he can make money by booking a few of the players himself. He might even offer a discount on the juice, since he doesn't have the overhead of a regular bookie. By booking players in the game, he can get his sports fix and also make some money.

However, he may not have the advantage he thinks he has. Line-making is a very sophisticated business in the Internet age. Let's assume he is lucky enough to avoid knowledgeable bettors. Some players may call him at late hours, interfering with his life and his rest schedule. They figure they deserve this kind of service, since he is charging juice. While our player-bookie pays the players who beat him, the players who are losing start making increasingly frequent bets until they owe more than they can pay. Some of them may have won money from him in previous weeks, but have spent it or lost it at poker or betting sports. Soon the player-bookie has a ledger of money he is owed. He is not skilled at debt collection. Some of his customers keep betting as long as they are winning. The losers go back to betting with regular bookies as they did before they got involved with our player-bookie.

There are worse things that can happen to the player-bookie than losing money. Bookmaking is a crime. The penalties differ from state to state. But if the bookie has five or more people helping him take bets and collect money, the crime may qualify under the guidelines of a state or federal Racketeering, Influence, and Corrupt Organization Act (RICO). A prison sentence of 10 to15 years is a possible consequence.

Here are some stories about poker players who got into other gambling situations, with the chance of winning a little or losing a lot.

Story 1: 1974, Northern California. A poker player who often bet on horses inherited $250,000. Another player proposed to book his bets and give him slightly better odds than he could get at the track. After a few weeks, the one doing the booking had all the money. He invested his profits in a business and never reentered the gambling world. He later confided to a friend that the first race was a 12 to 1 shot, and if the horse had won he couldn't have paid off the bet. His scheme would then have come to an abrupt end.

Story 2: 1975, Las Vegas. Sarge Ferris, a high-stakes poker player, shot pool with someone who had very little money. After they had been playing for a while, a friend whispered to Sarge, "This guy's got $200 to his name. You can't beat him out of anything." Sarge replied, "Yes, I can. He's got $40,200 now."

Story 3: 1993, Las Vegas. A wealthy poker player shot pool with a dice player who had borrowed a few thousand dollars and then took on a couple of partners. They started at $5000 per game and ended up playing for $20,000 per game. The dice player won about $300,000 for the session. When they left the pool hall, the poker player's car wouldn't start. The dice player gave him a ride back to his house in a wheezing, dilapidated old car. The guard at the gated community where the wealthy player lived wouldn't let the car through.

They played several other times, increasing the stakes along the way. Over the course of a month, the dice player had won about $2,000,000 before the poker player quit. He used this money to shoot craps at various casinos and play big-limit heads-up poker. Within two months, the dice player amassed a fortune of over $30,000,000. He owned almost all the $5000 chips at Binion's Horseshoe Casino, which he kept in several safety deposit boxes. But before the year was over, he had lost it all at craps and poker.

CHAPTER 14

PROTECTING YOURSELF

"Trust everybody, but cut the cards."

Finley Peter Dunne
(1867-1936),
American journalist and humorist

Ace on the River

THERE MAY BE NO ONE ELSE LOOKING OUT FOR YOU.

Generally speaking, poker games are honest. As in any business, however, when there is money to be made or lost, not everyone can be trusted. Protecting yourself from being cheated may seem a daunting task. Your main defense against cheating is your poker sense. Even in life outside of poker, you will continually be evaluating new situations and new people that you have to deal with. You build a mental list of people who are trustworthy and people to stay away from. I have been invited to games in small towns only to find out that the rake is prohibitive, the cards may be marked, or the dealers don't shuffle well. When I have asked players why they put up with these conditions, I have sometimes received the response, perhaps as a joke, "It's the only game in town."

There is no reason to invite danger. If you play in a casino, use chips instead of cash. When you cash out, put the money on deposit or in a safety deposit box. Don't do anything to suggest to total strangers that you carry a lot of cash with you. If you live in an area where poker is usually played in casinos, you should be suspicious of home games. Wherever you are, if you're invited to a home game, it is safer if you know some of the players, or at least that people you trust endorse the game.

If you play in an environment with many onlookers, check your rear-view mirror when you drive home to make sure you are not being followed. Carry a cell phone with you in case someone unexpected is waiting for you when you get home.

Even if you play in a casino, marked cards can be brought in. A floor-man can assist in bringing in a stacked deck and the dealer can make a false shuffle and cut, all to set you up to lose a big hand. Cameras with special hookups, electronic devices for pulse signaling, or earpieces can be used to cheat you. Your main protection will be your accurate evaluation of the people you play with and your awareness when you are losing in strange ways. Of course, weak players often think they are losing in strange ways.

Playing in games with surveillance cameras is helpful, but you should realize that one of the main purposes of surveillance is to protect the casino, not the patrons. Casinos have elaborate systems to double-check transactions and make it harder for employees to steal from the casino. Surveillance is used to protect the players, but mainly because it is good

Protecting Yourself

business for the casinos to give the impression that they have an honest place to play. High-stakes games are the most scrutinized because there is more money at risk and high-stakes players pay the highest time. When a cheating incident is uncovered, the cardroom managers normally handle it very discreetly. They are reluctant to publicize the details since they may be held liable for slander if they are unable to adequately prove their findings in court, and they fear that customers will wrongly assume that cheating is much more widespread than this isolated incident.

Players who are not in a hand have been known to cheat by using signals to indicate cards or strength of an opponent's hand to a partner who is in the hand. Use two hands to protect your hole cards. If you don't carefully prevent your hole cards from flashing, you may find that your opponents often make perfect plays against you.

Players may team up and use signals to indicate that a partner with a weak hand should raise and trap opponents in the middle. Even with no signaling, they can let only the apparent best hand of the partnership go against an outsider so he doesn't get multi-way action on his money. There is less chance of collusion and other forms of cheating at high-stakes poker, because the players in the game are more skilled at detecting what makes sense in the betting and what doesn't. Also, since there aren't many high-stakes players, it is easier to know about possible alliances. As players move up the ranks to the highest-limit games, they have to demonstrate their integrity. A winning player who takes cheap shots or doesn't play fair will be ostracized.

When the stakes get high, it can be difficult to find enough players to fill up the game. Sometimes one player may take a piece of another player, or even stake someone in the same game. This will add another player who otherwise would not be able to play at that limit. At other times, two players in the game are known to be close friends, but they have no financial agreement. Instead of assuming there is collusion, you should assess how it affects you. If they are doing something that is to your disadvantage, you may have to complain or quit. If they have alerted the table of their alliance and are honorable people who won't do anything that could look unethical, you can exploit them. Their hands will normally be more readable. When one of them raises his friend with other players in the pot, he will have a solid hand so he can show they were on the up-and-up. But be on the watch for one betting and the other calling, where the second player has a monster but doesn't want to isolate against his friend.

In tournaments, some players swap pieces with others. They may play soft against each other. Players with big stacks may throw off chips to players with small stacks expecting the favor to be returned later. One thousand out of a forty thousand dollar tournament stack will probably have no effect. But one thousand added to a one thousand dollar stack can make a big difference. There is not much you can do to protect yourself here, except for complaining if you see anything unethical happening.

Players have been known to pocket chips from their large stacks in one event to add to their short stacks in another event. Also, chips that have previously been stolen, with or without inside assistance from casino personnel, may be added to a player's stack. There have been some instances where tournament personnel have pocketed a portion of the rebuy money. None of these things happen frequently, but you should make sure that the total chips add up correctly at the final table.

If you play on the Internet and are never able to get away with a bluff against certain opponents, you may wonder if they have software enabling them to see your hands. You should make sure you have a firewall, which is software that restricts outside access to your computer. There is no way you can prevent your opponents from colluding by discussing their hands with each other via telephone or private messaging while they are playing online at the same table. Players are also capable of having multiple accounts and using two of them to play in the same game. The faster the game proceeds, the less likely it is that this type of collusion is occurring. If you think the play on some hands is suspicious, check the hand records, which are available to Internet players. If you are losing consistently when you play on the Internet, you should quit. This is the best protection you have against any form of collusion.

There is one item that won't be stolen from a poker room. You can leave a book and come back the next day and it will still be there, unless it is relevant to gambling.

CHAPTER 15

POKER
AND
YOUR
FAMILY

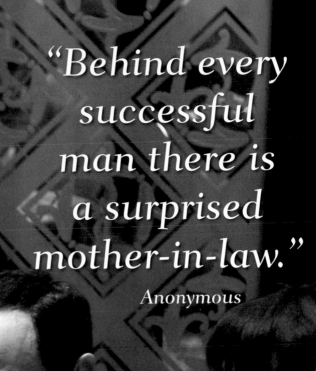

"Behind every successful man there is a surprised mother-in-law."

Anonymous

"None but a mule denies his family."

Arabian proverb

Ace on the River

I call the activities I engage in to provide for my family "work." Children watch the behavior of their parents. My children can see my behavior when I'm at home, but they only have a general idea of what I do when I'm working. If they think I just "play" cards for a living, they will have trouble understanding why I want them to work hard at their studies. Also, they will tend to become materialistic because, in their view, my job consists of only chasing money and is not associated with any tangible service, benefit, or product.

I don't invite people to my home to play poker. I wouldn't want my children to observe poker-table antics or get confused by the amount of money that is being thrown around. It might make it more difficult to teach them about sportsmanship and money. I am also careful about which of my "colleagues" come to my home and meet my children. Some players don't modify their anti-social behavior when they leave the poker table.

A professional poker player should be well-prepared to teach his children about honor, integrity, and playing within a set of rules. However, some problems may arise that do not have obvious solutions. When one of my children was in second grade he had to demonstrate to the class what his father did for a living. I told him I invest in the stock market, which was true, but deceptive. Also, during a time of disharmony in my marriage, another child came to me and said, "Mommy says you're just a gambler. Is that true, and what is that?"

Expert poker players excel at a game that rewards deception and the ability to bluff. It would not be surprising to find that the children of professional poker players tell more lies than other children. But a good poker player will often detect their lies, as he is adept at dealing with misleading information. Naturally, it is his job as a parent to teach his children not to lie.

One benefit of being a poker player is that I am my own boss and can take off from work when I want to. I use this freedom to enhance the life of my family. I don't play poker when I have promised to spend time with them. It is not good for them, and it is a distraction that can affect how well I play. In addition, if I played and lost, I would feel much worse than

I would otherwise. But when the going is rough, it's hard to devote as much time to my family as I should.

If you are aware that your partner will punish you with verbal abuse or neglect when you lose, this may influence you to make bad decisions. When you should quit, you may stay and try to get even to avoid an argument when you get home. Also, you will tend to guard small wins when you should be aggressively seeking a big score. Ideally, you want a partner who is happy when you win, but consoles you when you lose. However, if your spouse finds it difficult to tolerate the ups and downs that you have trained yourself to handle, perhaps you can discuss this problem with her and persuade her not to take each loss too seriously.

Traveling long hours to play poker can cause your level of play to decline. When I began playing regularly in southern California, I knew I needed to move closer to where I worked, just as I would have for any other job. Even if you move close to the most frequent location of your games, there will still be times when you have to travel, especially if you play in tournaments. If you have the benefit of your spouse traveling with you, it will be difficult to arrange your poker schedule so you can spend time with her. Bringing children along can further complicate matters. They will feel that they are on vacation and will expect more of your time than you can give them.

Poker and Your Family

Players who play most of their poker online have the advantage of spending a lot of time at home. Unfortunately, playing poker all day while ignoring one's spouse and children is worse than not being home. Your lack of attention will wear on them, and your frustration over losses will be more evident when you don't have the cooling off period afforded during the drive home. Also, since children copy adults, your children will probably spend a lot of time playing card games and may possibly even play poker on the computer.

The job of a professional poker player is much like that of a salesman who works on commission. Sometimes money comes in bunches, and sometimes there's a negative cash flow. During the negative periods, spending should be kept to a minimum. When I have money, I pay my bills and debts first. If I still have enough left to weather a losing streak, I am extravagant with my family and friends. In flush times it is easy to be careless about spending money. There is a tendency to spoil your children with gifts when times are good to make up for not spending time with them when you were struggling. I have learned from experience that it is better to pamper them with time. They will remember time spent with their father long after the toys and trinkets are gone.

CHAPTER 16

POKER
AND
YOUR
SEXUALITY

"I have looked on a lot of women with lust. I've committed adultery in my heart many times."

Jimmy Carter
(1924-),
39th president of the
United States

"God gave men both a penis and a brain, but unfortunately not enough blood supply to run both at the same time."

Robin Williams
(1952-),
American comedian

UNDERSTANDING YOUR BIOLOGICAL NATURE
WILL LEAD TO BETTER RESULTS.

Casinos hire good-looking employees to attract and distract customers. Like a corollary to Murphy's Law, the number of people you are sexually attracted to, but cannot have, is proportional to your level of sexual frustration. Studies show that the frequency of sexual thoughts when we are awake or asleep is correlated with the level of our sexual frustration. If you are sexually frustrated, you may have trouble concentrating on poker.

Having a sexual desire for someone you find physically attractive is a normal biological reaction. Players often say, "It's the chase that I like." Maybe what they really like is *being* chased. It is flattering that someone you hardly know is willing to go to bed with you, but you are fooling yourself. It is far more satisfying when someone who knows you as a person is interested in you, than when a woman is pursuing you for your "pocket charm" because it will enhance her gambling career.

Chips of large denomination can have an aphrodisiac effect. In the casino society, where everything gets reduced to its monetary value, sex is often just another commodity. In order to get sex, some men prey on women who are in need of money. They may try to speed up the casual sex cycle by introducing drugs and alcohol. Many players quit good games to chase women and spend a lot of money to satisfy

Poker and Your Sexuality

their sexual desires. This can lead to serious financial consequences, not to mention the health risks associated with drugs and alcohol. In these encounters, the predator may become the prey if one partner in the relationship is in need of financial support. Becoming a sugar daddy can have a devastating effect on one's gambling bankroll. Complete honesty with yourself and awareness that you have these sexual cravings may help you to avoid some of these pitfalls or prevent them from getting out of hand.

Sexual frustration occurs more frequently in males than in females, but women players may also use sex for relaxation. In addition, women on the road are more likely to seek friendship since they tend to share their feelings more freely than men do.

If you have sex before you go to sleep, you probably will be more rested and less distracted when you play. Therefore, a sex partner who travels with you can be a big asset. In theory, if your partner isn't with you when you go on an extended poker trip out of town, a relatively steady substitute will give you a competitive advantage. Some spouses of athletes and politicians may accept this as part of the territory, but poker players don't have that kind of status.

CHAPTER 17

THE BEST
POKER
PLAYER
IN THE
WORLD

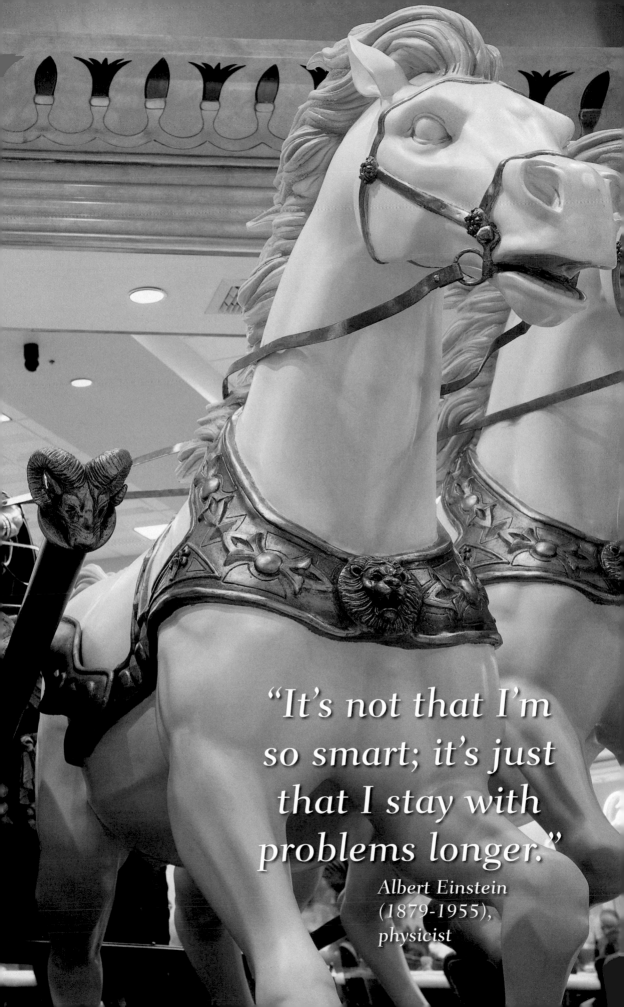

"It's not that I'm so smart; it's just that I stay with problems longer."

Albert Einstein
(1879-1955),
physicist

Ace on the River

If you privately ask the regulars in a poker game who is the best player in their game, each one may tell you that he is. This view of himself is based on the times when he is playing his best. He may try to justify his opinion by pointing out one aspect of the game that he values highly and in which he believes he is better than the others. Of course, each player may have a different perception as to which element of the game is the most important. But until we observe a player when he is losing and hav-

The Best Poker Player in the World

ing a bad run of cards, we don't have an accurate picture of how good he really is. Handling adversity is a key component of being a good poker player.

I have spent some time thinking about who is the best player in the world. I have played poker at the highest levels, and I believe I know the answer. Is it one of the top tournament players? As Deep Throat said in *All the President's Men*, "Follow the money." If tournament players are that good, they would be winning millions of dollars in high-stakes games. Higher-limit players wish tournament players would take their winnings and jump into the big games. Some of them have tried that, but most have not been successful even at the middle limits.

Are *you* the best? It is unlikely that you are the one. Am I the best? You haven't seen some of the dumb plays I have made over the years. I have been outplayed thousands of times. I have often fallen into traps set by weak players. As a matter of fact, I have been able to write this book because I have a good memory for many of the stupid things I have done and continue to do.

So how do we judge who is the best? Is it the player who wins the most money? He may have a lifestyle strategy which enables him to get into the best situations, but he may be unable to beat the toughest games. We might say he is the most effective player. Even if we consider game selection an important component in choosing the best player, we should give some consideration to a winning player who has a life outside of poker that prevents him from doing a lot of traveling. If he can't find large games to build up his bankroll, he won't be able to afford to play in the biggest games. Consequently, he can't make the most money.

The best player could be someone who wins consistently at the stakes he plays, but doesn't want to risk going broke in the highest-limit games.

Also, we may consider players who are great at poker but are broke because they are self-destructive in other facets of their lives. Of course, there are also the self-proclaimed best players in the world who believe that any game in which they lose is crooked, and who suspect that the winners in the bigger-stakes games are cheating.

Thousands of decisions are made every time one sits down to play poker. If we tried to judge a player on his percentage of right and wrong decisions, we would have to place greater weight on some decisions than on others. Whether to sit in the game at all probably should be weighted many more times than whether to check or bet on a particular hand. What to say, how to act, all the things I have discussed require decisions. It is impossible to evaluate, but we may guess that the top players have a 90% rating and, of course, weaker players would have a lower rating. It is not humanly possible to do everything right all the time.

To complicate matters, some players do better against one set of opponents and some do better against another. The most prominent example of this occurs when tournament players are compared to side-game players. The top tournament players are proficient at extracting the maximum from the weaker opponents they face in a large tournament, but their own weaknesses might be exploited if they sat down with top side-game players.

Some players are better at one type of poker than at another. Some are better at certain variations of a game. For

The Best Poker Player in the World

example, some top stud players are good as long as the ante-to-small-bet ratio is 1 : 4 or 1 : 5, but they become live ones if the ante is lower. Also, some players are better short-handed than in a ring game.

Even heads-up, when Player A is a favorite over Player B, and Player B is a favorite over Player C, Player A may *not* be a favorite over Player C. This frequently happens in sports because some defenses are better than others against certain offenses. In poker, because of differences in style, the same principle applies.

In any case, it would not be a relevant factor in a player's moneymaking ability if it were somehow decided that he was 0.1% better than another player. Money is made as a result of having a substantial advantage over the weaker players in a game. The only reason a player might want to consider himself the best is to soothe his weak ego.

So, who is the best player in the world? The answer is: No one. Nobody plays his or her best every day. No player is the best in all forms of poker against all groups of opponents on an everyday basis. Even in your poker circle, you are not going to be the best all the time. Just try to play well and manage well.

CHAPTER 18

GAMBLING
AND
PRODUCTIVE
SOCIETY

"The best way to get a bad law repealed is to enforce it strictly."

Abraham Lincoln
(1809-1865),
16th president of
the United States

"The gambling known as business looks with severe disfavor on the business known as gambling."

Ambrose Bierce
(1842-1914),
American author

POKER HAS TAUGHT ME TO ANALYZE ISSUES FROM DIFFERENT PERSPECTIVES.

It may well be said that gambling, not prostitution, is the oldest profession. Prehistoric man could have survived on nuts, fruits, plants, and meat from small animals, but the risk-takers of that era gambled, with their lives on the line, for the big kill. Soon after cattle and crops became a form of currency, gambling games followed. The wheel was invented some time later, perhaps when a lucky gambler needed a way to cart his winnings back to his cave.

Colored pebbles and particular kinds of bones of animals were found in Egyptian and Babylonian sites, circa 3600 B.C. The bones were from just above the heel bones of sheep, deer, and other animals. Archeologists suspect that the pebbles were playing pieces and the bones were used as randomizing devices. The four "random" outcomes were the four possible orientations in which a bone might fall when it was flung to the ground. Gambling artifacts have been recovered from China, circa 2300 B.C., and also from a later time in India, Egypt, and Rome. A set of ivory dice from around 1500 B.C. was salvaged from the ancient Egyptian city of Thebes,

and gambling was mentioned on a tablet found in the Pyramid of Cheops in Egypt.

Gambling has been the genesis for many mathematical ideas. Girolamo Cardano, credited with being the father of probability, wrote *Liber de Ludo Aleae* (The Book on Games of Chance) in 1520. He was a losing gambler who used his mathematical ability to figure out why he lost. Other famous mathematicians have made major contributions that arose from questions about gambling games. In 1654, Blaise Pascal had a lengthy correspondence about gambling odds for dice games with Pierre de Fermat which launched the next major advance in the field of probability. Pascal's pioneering work on binomial coefficients resulted from this correspondence. The definitive works on gambling for their times were *De Ratiociniis in Ludo Aleae* (On Reasoning in Games of Chance) by Christiaan Huygens in 1657, *Arts Conjectandi* (Art of Guessing) by Jakob Bernoulli in 1713, and *Theory of Games and Economic Behavior* by John von Neumann and Oskar Morgenstern in 1944.

Gambling has had an indirect effect on literature. Fyodor Dostoyevsky and Edgar Allen Poe often wrote to support their gambling habits. If Dostoyevsky had taken more than a month to write *The Gambler*, he would have had to pay royalties for all of his subsequent works to a person to

Ace on the River

whom he owed money from his roulette losses. Poe dropped out of the University of Virginia in 1827 because of mounting gambling debts. He was a heavy drinker who gambled when he drank. He became a master at writing about terror and sorrow, conditions resulting from his gambling losses.

Many authors portray the gambler as a romantic figure who is able to survive on his wits. Gambling represents a level playing field for conflict between common people and the affluent. Even stories from the Old West distinguish the gambler from the hustler: the white hat, a man of his word, versus the black hat, a cheating scoundrel without moral redemption.

Gambling is an expression of freedom in oppressed societies. When the communist North Vietnamese seized the South in 1975, they prohibited free enterprise, freedom of religion, and freedom of speech. They were unsuccessful at suppressing the open gambling in which many Vietnamese traditionally participate during the first week of the New Year. In other restricted environments, gambling is a liberating activity. Mental hospitals take patients out for "Gambling Day" at the local casinos. Such trips provided material for Ken Kesey's *One Flew Over the Cuckoo's Nest* after his stay in a psychiatric ward. In the armed forces, many soldiers look forward to gambling during the first few days after the monthly paychecks arrive.

Wherever casinos and betting parlors are not legal, they are run privately. Many restaurants in ethnic neighborhoods have a back room featuring gambling games of the culture. The prevalence of gambling seems to

Gambling and Productive Society

be correlated with the level of superstition in the culture. Even the poorest countries have a numbers racket in which a player wins if his number matches an agreed-upon daily variable. In many cases, the last three digits of the total amount wagered at a given racetrack are used. Anyone can find those in the sports pages. If the numbers racket is government sanctioned, the payout is usually around 500 to 1. Illegal operations typically pay 600 to 1.

Gambling is the essence of capitalism. Inventors and entrepreneurs stake their future on new products and new ways of doing business. Investors bet on others' ideas and those with quick wits and market savvy get rich. Capitalism rewards competition, which increases productivity and creates better products. The side effect is the creation of an economic class system, as successful investors and entrepreneurs make big money from other people's work. Gamblers also take a piece of the profits made from the labor of others.

Casinos are an integral part of the new global economy. Consider any locality that has authority to determine the legality of casino gambling. These localities may be cities, states, provinces, or countries. I will call them *jurisdictions* to point out their self-governing capability with respect to gambling. If a jurisdiction has a weak economy and is in close proximity to a jurisdiction that produces a significantly-sized middle and upper class, but has no legalized casinos, there will be casinos across the border. Some examples are Native American reservations, Windsor across the border from Detroit, Cambodia on the Thai border, Monte Carlo between France and Italy, and Sun City in southern Africa. We can include riverboat casinos and casinos on island nations, such as the Bahamas, Aruba, and the Mediterranean island of Cyprus. In many places the indigenous people are not allowed to play, supposedly to protect them from being victimized by gambling. Actually, the practice is usually an act of discrimination designed to keep the local "undesirables" out of the

Gambling and Productive Society

casinos. The benefits the local people may derive from tax revenue pale in comparison to the profits shared by the casino operators and government officials.

Whenever governments are involved, the odds tend to be worse and the public is hustled the most. People are lured by the slim chance of a big payoff for a small price with no effort or skill required on their part. Unfortunately, this usually creates a culture of depressed, uneducated, addicted gamblers. The downtrodden losers become fatalists who believe that they are losers in life and think their gambling results prove that point. Most people don't understand that they are losing because of the mathematical nature of the game, not because of their own bad karma. State and federal gambling entities should publicize the odds, which would at least serve to educate the populace about their mathematical chances. Lotteries and casino gambling should be promoted as entertainment, not as a chance for someone to solve a financial crisis.

Horse tracks around the world take out an average of around 20% of the total handle. Off-track and illegal bookmakers often pay better. Lotteries pay back as little as 25 cents on the dollar, and some of that money is paid over time and taxed heavily. To generate more interest, lotteries are changed periodically so that the maximum payout is increased and the percentage paid back is decreased.

Lottery slogans often target compulsive people. In many states the slogan is "You can't win if you don't play." Here are some other examples:

California: "Don't let your number win without you."
New York: "All you need is a dollar and a dream."
England: "It could be you."
South Africa: "Tata ma chance, tata ma millions."

I don't know what *tata ma* means, but *millions* is the word that gets gullible lottery players lining up to buy tickets, no matter how remote the odds.

Some slogans promote the lottery as a civic duty.

Tennessee: "Leave no child behind! Just leave your money behind!"
China: "Liguo liji," which means "Benefit the nation, benefit yourself."
Kenya: "Everyone is a winner."

The implication is that lottery revenue helps everyone.

Ace on the River

When jurisdictions try to solve their financial problems, gambling is often considered as a source of income. Lobbyists appeal to voters by promising that gambling revenue will prevent tax increases and create a windfall for the education budget. In reality, if a gambling referendum passes, only part of the new income is allotted for education and funds that previously went to education are cut from the original budget, so the money ends up about the same. The main beneficiaries are lobbyists, gambling organizers, and politicians whose campaigns were funded and whose pockets were greased to support the initiative.

Aside from gambling referenda, there are often measures on the ballot that deal with instituting tax increases, reapportioning funds from the budget, or enacting new laws. The opposing sides use dizzying rhetoric to explain that if you vote their way, money will be saved in the long run and things will be better for you and your family and worse for some special interest group. My gambling training has taught me to be leery of people who are trying to hustle me into doing something they say is good for me, when the only thing I know for sure is that it's good for them. Therefore, I try to understand the agenda of special interest groups, and I seek advice from nonpartisan groups whose research I trust and whose positions I'm comfortable with before I cast my vote.

I am always suspicious of the motives of companies that push dangerous products and at the same time warn against them. Alcohol companies responded to statistics showing 40% of fatal accidents involve a drunk driver by including "Drink Responsibly" or "Don't Drink and Drive" at the end of their hard-sell advertising. While tobacco companies were forced to print "Smoking may be hazardous to your health" on cigarette packages, these disclaimers served as a defense in court against lawsuits by lung cancer victims. Organized gambling ventures endeavor to entice people to gamble but fool them about the odds. Then they pretend they are socially conscious by providing brochures with the phone number of Gambler's Anonymous and messages such as "Bet with your head, not over it."

I have felt a need to justify my role in society. I like to think of myself as a modern-day Robin Hood. By using my wits, I take money from rich people for the benefit of others. I provide comfort and security for my family and I also help the needy. Giving to charity is my way of doing something constructive with this inherently nonproductive profession. Since I use the highways, the schools, the police, and the fire department, I pay my share of taxes and am not a burden on society. I take liberal deductions for my expenses, but I sleep well at night knowing I am a respon-

Gambling and Productive Society

sible citizen. When I lose or incur a bad debt, I can console myself with the knowledge that the government is my partner in that also. Instead of stashing my money away in cash and avoiding luxuries I can afford, I employ and provide for others, put aside sufficient money for my future needs, and live well.

PART III

ADVANCED

PLAY

CHAPTER 19

MATHEMATICS

OF

POKER

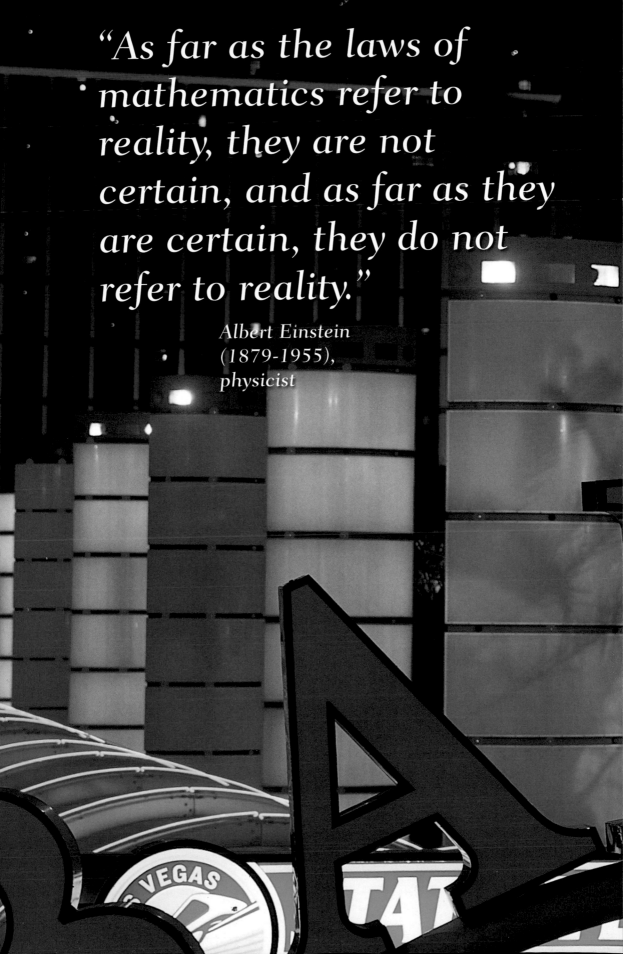

"As far as the laws of mathematics refer to reality, they are not certain, and as far as they are certain, they do not refer to reality."

Albert Einstein
(1879-1955),
physicist

Ace on the River

HOW MUCH MATH IS REQUIRED TO BECOME A GOOD PLAYER?

It is not necessary to be good at mathematics to become a good poker player. It is helpful, however, to be able to think logically and to be good at solving problems, which are important mathematical skills. The mathematics used for no-limit and pot-limit poker is simple arithmetic. Even that knowledge is unnecessary to play limit poker. Instead of using mathematics to determine which hands to play, players rely on memorized strategies acquired from reading or experience.

The most frequent calculation I do involves figuring out my position when no one has entered into the pot on the first betting round. Occasionally, I have mistakenly thought I was in early position, but after throwing away my hand, I realized one player went to the bathroom, another was dealt out of the hand, a player to my left was folding before it was his turn to act, and therefore I was actually in middle or late position. Of course, many more hands are playable in late position than early position because there are fewer chances of having a good hand out against you among the players left to act. Also, you will usually have the advantage of acting after your opponents in subsequent betting rounds.

It will occasionally be helpful if you can count the number of outs you have and are able to figure out pot odds in simple situations. In limit poker, you will generally continue on in a hand when you have eight outs or more.

Mathematics of Poker

SOME USEFUL MATHEMATICAL FACTS YOU SHOULD KNOW

Hold'em:

If you flop a flush or a straight draw, with no other ways of winning, you are approximately a 2 to 1 underdog.

If you have a small pair and need to make trips to win, you will not have sufficient pot odds in limit hold'em to take a card off on the turn.

If you have 13 outs on the flop, you will typically be a slight underdog.

If you have 14 outs on the flop, you will typically be a slight favorite.

A big pocket pair against a small pocket pair is slightly more than a 4 to 1 favorite to win the hand.

If you have a pocket pair, you are around a 7.5 to 1 underdog to flop a set.

Seven-card stud:

If you have an open-end straight draw or a flush draw in the first four cards, you will typically be a slight underdog to make the hand. Of course, you may win by making something other than the straight or flush, or you may win by playing aggressively.

A starting three-card straight has about an even chance of winning against an underpair with a small kicker if there is no betting after the first three cards.

Lowball:

Against a one-card draw, in Ace-to-Five lowball,
        a pat Nine is typically a 1.8 to 1 favorite,
        a pat Ten is typically a slight favorite,
        a pat Jack is typically a slight underdog.

In Deuce-to-Seven lowball, the same can be said about pat Tens, pat Jacks, and pat Queens, respectively.

If Ace-to-Five lowball is played with the joker and the drawing
hand holds the joker, a smooth one-card draw with the joker
is typically a slight underdog against a pat Nine and a slight
favorite against a pat Ten.

Pot-limit Omaha:

A hand with two Aces is a favorite against all hands that do not
have two Aces, except in a few rare cases. The worst case is
A♠ A♥ 6♦ 2♣ vs. J♠ 10♠ 9♥ 8♥. In this match-up, the hand
with the Aces wins about 49% of the time.

A set is normally a favorite against a complete wrap on the flop.

A flush draw is normally a favorite against a complete wrap on the
flop.

Mathematics of Poker

Other gambling games:

If you are in a gambling situation where you have the worst of it, no betting strategy will make you a favorite. For example, there is no betting system to beat the casinos at craps.

You can play with a betting strategy that will allow you to win a high percentage of the time, but in the long run you will still lose. You will have many small wins, but your big losses will be more than the sum of the small wins. The typical strategy used is akin to what is called a Martingale Strategy .

Definition of Martingale Strategy: Make a small bet. If you win, quit. If you lose, bet the amount you are behind plus enough for a small profit. Repeat the process until you win.

Many players manage their poker sessions using a Martingale approach. They hit and run with small wins, but if they are losing they play until they drop. They are psychologically fulfilled 90% of the time, but they still lose money overall.

Even though betting strategies will not counteract a mathematical disadvantage, you may lose money to someone employing a Martingale type strategy against you. For example, let's say someone allows you to flip a coin, and he will always call heads and will pay you 2 to 1 odds. He gets to decide the amount to bet on each flip and how many times to flip, each time paying 2 to 1 odds. He guarantees that he will do this with you every day, and that he will never try to beat you out of more than $100 for the day. There is no settling up until he calls it quits for the day.

His system: Bet to win $100 the first flip; if he loses, he will be down $200, so he will bet to win $300 on the next flip. If he keeps losing, he will bet an amount that will let him win $100. The sequence of bets will be $100, $300, $900, $2700, and so on. If heads comes up on the nth flip, he will have bet $100 x 3 $^{(n-1)}$ on that flip, and he will now quit and collect his $100 for the day. There may be some long streaks of tails and he may get up to amounts he cannot pay, but eventually heads will hit and he will collect $100. If casinos gave unlimited credit and allowed unlimited bets, they would all go broke. But of course, there are credit limits and table limits.

When we use mathematics for real world applications, we make a model of a situation and then make computations based on that model. There are models for the stock market, for analyzing sporting events, and for figuring the odds at poker. The mathematics is always right, but we have to make sure the model is relevant in the real world. As in the previous example, following a model that gives us a positive expectation may still result in a loss of money.

If someone is losing and wants to increase the stakes, you may think, "I have an edge now. I can make twice as much." Don't let him do this on credit if he is going to get into amounts he can't pay. Don't let him do this if you think he will start playing significantly better, now that it is easier for him to get out of the trap.

SOME INTERESTING BUT NOT TOO USEFUL MATHEMATICAL FACTS:

In hold'em, with no betting after the flop, all pairs are a favorite over Ace-King offsuit, by at least 52% to 48%. All pairs except Deuces with neither card in the Ace-King's suit are favored over Ace-King suited. If several players fold first, Ace-King suited is a favorite over most pairs. (The exceptions are Aces, Kings, and Jacks, and also Tens where one of the Tens is the same suit as the Ace-King.) Even Ace-King offsuit is now a favorite against small pairs. The reason for this is that players are more likely to play hands having an Ace or King than those containing smaller cards. Therefore, as players fold, the probability of an Ace or King coming on the board increases.

The chances of having pocket Aces in hold'em are 1 in 221. When everyone folds to you and you have the big blind, the probability of having a pair of Aces is approximately 1 in 134, since players are more likely to enter the pot if they have an Ace.

Similarly, but more obviously, when everyone folds to the big blind in lowball, it is likely that the big blind will pick up a hand mainly consisting of low cards.

When playing heads-up triple-draw lowball, it shouldn't be surprising that pat hands get beat on the third draw much more frequently than in single draw, since some useless cards have been discarded on the first two draws, and the opponent is drawing to better hands.

Two players play a heads-up session for eight hours. Let's suppose they play 40 hands per hour for a total of 320 hands. If every hand has a 50% chance to be won by one player or the other, what is the average longest winning streak either of them will have?

Mathematics of Poker

If n is the number of hands, the average longest streak is approximately $\log_2 n$, even for small values of n. We should expect, on average, that one player will win eight hands in a row over the course of 320 hands. People tend to expect things to even out sooner than they do, so they are surprised by the streaks that come about. This leads them to believe that other things must be influencing the results: "He's just hot," "That's his lucky dealer," etc.

MISUSING MATHEMATICS

I have heard people say, "I had to call with a lousy hand because I was getting 5 to 1 on my money," not taking into account that they were up against five opponents with better hands than they had. For example, if you hold 5♥ 2♥ in hold'em, it might be right to call against one player if a lot of extra money was magically added to the pot. Against five players, however, you may lose with a small flush to a bigger flush or make two pair and be up against three Fives. There are more ways to lose when you are up against more hands.

Players sometimes say they called because of the implied odds, which takes into account action they were going to get if they made their hand. Often, they had no reason to expect they were going to get that kind of action. Also, they don't take into account that if they made the hand, it still

might not end up being the winner. It is usually right to fold if it was a borderline decision even after accounting for the implied odds. However, when you analyze the situation, you sometimes realize that your opponent probably isn't going to be able to call your raise when you make the hand. If you come to the conclusion that he may be too weak to call a raise even now, then you should raise with your draw as a back-up way of winning the hand.

When players get beat with the best hand, they sometimes spout mathematical nonsense about how big a favorite they were. For example, when they lose with Ace-King against King-Jack in hold'em, you may hear them complain that they got beat by a three-outer and were a 45 to 3 favorite. In reality, they were between a 2.3 to 1 favorite and a 3.1 to 1 favorite, depending on the suits.

Story 1: In 1992, I was playing in the best $75-$150 hold'em game in which I had ever played. One player was playing like such a maniac that he raised before the flop every time it was his turn. If it was two bets to him, he made it three bets. If it was three bets to him, he made it four bets, which was the cap. After a few rounds, the other players knew not to raise with their good hands. They would limp in, try to trap a few callers, and wait for the maniac's raise and then they would reraise. A well-known

poker writer was sitting to the maniac's right. For seven consecutive rounds, the poker writer called in the small blind only to be knocked out before the flop when the maniac raised and some other player reraised. The maniac went broke after the seventh round of this, so I don't know how long this would have gone on. I was surprised that the poker writer, a supposedly winning player, had so little table feel. He must have played using strictly memorized guidelines. He would look at his hand, let's say 10♥ 4♥ or Q♠ 8♦, and after consulting his mental chart, he would decide that the hand was worth a call in the small blind. Then, when it came back to him, he would decide the hand did not qualify for two more bets.

Story 2: In 1975, while I was attending college, I played dealer's choice with college students, locals, and a philosophy professor. The minimum buy-in was $20, but towards the end of the night, players would typically have a couple of hundred in front of them. One night, the professor and I had been killing the game, and we each had around $3000 in front of us.

The current game was pot-limit, seven-card stud hi-lo. I raised the bring-in $7, making the pot $28 after two of the other six players called on third street. A bet of $28 on fourth street got the pot down to heads-up between the professor and me. The pot was now $84. I bet $84 on fifth street and the professor called, making the pot $252. He bet $252 on sixth street. I hesitated and then called. On the river, he bet $750 and I raised the rest of his chips.

His board was

My board was

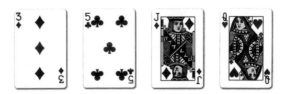

After a minute of studying, he flashed his hand to the table, showing a Six-high straight. He said, "The only way you can scoop me is if you have three low diamonds in the hole. I just figured out that the odds of that are much more than 1000 to 1 against, but you are so lucky, I think you've got it. But with those odds, I have to call." He put his money in and I showed him the A♦ 4♦ 6♦ out of the hole, giving me a better low and a flush.

The professor screamed at me, "You're a @#$% math genius. What do you think the odds were?"

I said, "It had to be close to a lock. I wouldn't have called a bet that big on sixth street without a two-way draw. When you bet on the river, I was pretty sure you had a straight. When I raised, it verified I had made both hands."

Story 3: Someone shows you a coin with a head and a tail on it. You watch him flip it ten times and all ten times it comes up heads. What is the probability that it will come up heads on the eleventh flip?

A novice gambler would tell you, "Tails is more likely than heads, since things have to even out and tails is due to come up."

A math student would tell you, "We can't predict the future from the past. The odds are still even."

A professional gambler would say, "There must be something wrong with the coin or the way it is being flipped. I wouldn't bet with the guy flipping it, but I'd bet someone else that heads will come up again."

CHAPTER 20

GAME
THEORY

"There's no sense in being precise when you don't even know what you're talking about."

John von Neumann
(1903-1957),
Hungarian-born American
mathematician and pioneer in
computers and game theory

Ace on the River

DOES KNOWLEDGE OF GAME THEORY SEPARATE THE TOP PLAYERS FROM THE REST?

Game theory is a branch of mathematics used to analyze competitive situations that depend not only on one's own choices, but also on the choices made by others. Some people have the mistaken perception that the ability to compute game theory and probability calculations separates expert players from the rest.

Quantitative knowledge of game theory is not necessary to become an expert poker player. However, qualitative concepts of game theory provide a framework for analyzing expert play and ideas. Similarly, you do not need to be an expert in psychology, although we can use psychology to explain how an expert poker player analyzes himself and his opponents.

There are two kinds of game theory, and both are relevant for the professional poker player. The first is cooperative game theory, which involves situations where more than one person has a common goal. In the case of poker, the goal is to keep a good game going for an extended period of time. The second kind is non-cooperative game theory, which we apply to maximize profits in an individual hand of poker.

SOME COOPERATIVE GAME THEORY STRATEGIES ARE:

1. Not quitting a game unless there are players to take your seat. If you hit-and-run, other players will do this in the future, and you will create an atmosphere in which the game is always in danger of breaking up.

2. Not antagonizing losing players. Even though it may make them play worse at this moment, they may not want to play in future poker games.

Game Theory

3. Not obsessively getting the best seat position. If you are jumping around the table, continually competing with other players for best position on live ones, you will make the game into a circus and cause the live ones to feel uncomfortable.

4. Compromising on which games to play and what stakes to play for. If you are a winning player and always have to have your way, people will avoid playing with you.

5. Not trying to beat a catalyst for as much money as possible in a session. Although it may be best to maximize your profit in the short term, you don't want to do anything that will cause this player to stop playing on a regular basis.

6. Not trying to convince a live one to quit when you aren't able to play. Some winning players are so afraid that someone else will win money when they aren't in the game, that they try to get the live ones to play only with them. This is very insulting to everybody. Weak players have often made money by being successful businessmen. They are not stupid people. They just aren't experts at poker.

♠♥♦♣

At the heart of non-cooperative game theory as it applies to playing poker is the concept that if you occasionally bluff, people will have to pay you off on your good hands. Game theoretical analysis focuses on determining the correct bluffing frequency to maximize profits. In game theory models, when two actions have the same expected value, some randomizing method is often used to determine which one to choose. This is a reasonable theory for a mathematical model, but in reality, no two situations are ever the same. There is always information swaying you in one direction or another, and

there is always an event history which includes plays that have been made on previous hands.

A GOOD PLAYER BLUFFS BASED ON:

1. Who he is playing against. Some opponents are more easily bluffed than others.

2. How strong he thinks his opponents' hands are.

3. What he has represented up to this point about the strength of his own hand.

4. Whether the opponent is in a calling mode. It is usually harder to bluff a loser, although some may be easier to bluff because they don't want to chase and lose again as they did on the last hand they played.

5. His chances of winning without bluffing.

6. The amount that will be gained by a successful bluff.

7. The probability that his opponent will counter with a raise-bluff or a check-raise-bluff.

8. The cards in his hand that his opponent would need to make a good hand.

9. His perceived table image. If he bluffs too much, other players will tend to call him down.

10. Situational reasons. a) The opponent is short of money and doesn't have any more to rebuy. b) The opponent doesn't want to call with a weak hand and look stupid in front of a friend or backer who is watching. c) In tournaments, it is easier to bluff right before a tournament break, immediately after the limits have been raised, or when there is a money increase for the next payout spot and the opponent is short on chips.

The same considerations apply when deciding whether to call with a weak hand if you think an opponent might be bluffing. Some players don't bluff in certain situations. For example, there are players who never raise-bluff. Other players must be called down with marginal hands due to the psychological state they are in.

When contemplating if you should call the final bet of a hand where you can only beat a bluff, you may make a pot-odds calculation. For example, in a limit game when you are getting 7 to 1 odds on a call, you might ask yourself if this opponent would try to bluff more than one time in eight if he didn't have a good hand. The answer will invariably be *yes*, but you must take into account that in many cases he is more than a 7 to 1 favorite to have a better hand than yours, based on the betting at previous points of the hand.

When considering whether to bluff for one bet at a pot with six bets in it, you have to decide if your opponent is likely to fold more than one time in seven. As you gain experience, you will become better at translating your poker sense into odds. Normally, you will not do any calculations. You will get a feel for the correct calling frequency in bluffing situations. If you continually find yourself in situations where you have to choose whether to bluff or call a possible bluff, you are probably making some bad decisions on earlier streets. An expert combines bluffing with frequent value-bets on marginal hands to break his opponents down to the point where they feel they have to call with anything.

I have occasionally been told that someone has come up with an optimal solution for playing a particular form of poker. The forms of poker that are commonly played are too complicated for this to be true. Someone may use win-rates for different hands to come up with a good strategy for the early betting rounds. But poker at a high level is a game of psychological adjustments, whether by using physical tells or by noticing opponents' patterns of playing certain types of hands over extended periods of time.

Game Theory

A beginner may ask himself, "What should I do with this hand?" He may view poker as a sequence of hands that are bet without regard to actions of his opponents. An intermediate player may ask the same question, but now incorporates bets that opponents have made. However, an advanced player will change the question to, "What should I do in this situation?" This question takes into account psychological aspects of poker with regard to his opponents, and also incorporates how he has played other hands. His plays are part of his overall system of play. Hands can no longer be thought of as isolated.

It would be difficult to play against a computerized opponent with a good strategy. The computer wouldn't steam or have tells like a live opponent. If I were to program a computer to play poker, I would use statistical rankings of hands, pot-odds decisions, and bluffing calculations based on principles of game theory. It is likely that a computer can be programmed using concepts of non-cooperative game theory to beat expert poker players, but it will be a long time before computers will be able to exploit weaker players as well as an expert can. Poker sense is hard to program.

CHAPTER 21

STUD

CHAOS

"Inevitably, underlying instabilities begin to appear. Flaws in the system will now become severe."

Ian Malcolm in Jurassic Park by Michael Crichton (1942-), American author

Ace on the River

RESULTS MAY BE UNPREDICTABLE.

If you knew, at each point on earth, every meteorological measurement — temperature, humidity, air pressure, wind direction, and any other quantity — and entered these into an infinitely powerful weather-predicting computer, you still would not be able to accurately predict the weather a month in the future. There are other factors in the weather system that may seem negligible, but as time goes on, their effects lead to unpredictable results. In the real world, the change in airflow from the flap of a butterfly's wings will contribute to minute differences in the meteorological measurements around the butterfly. These differences will upset the balance in an increasingly larger area as time passes. Theoretically, it is conceivable that the flap of a butterfly's wings in Brazil may set off a tornado in Texas, as mathematician Edward Lorenz suggested in a landmark lecture in December 1972. This example, called the Butterfly Effect, illustrates the impossibility of making predictions for complex systems, even though the systems are determined by underlying conditions. This is the premise of chaos theory, a relatively new branch of mathematics which involves the study of systems that are very sensitive to small changes in initial conditions.

As you walk up to the poker table, a hand is being dealt and you ask to get dealt in, but you are one second too late. While you have no way of knowing, you would have won that hand. But you lose the next hand, which would have never been dealt the way it was. A phone call a few tables away causes your next unforeseen disaster, because the recipient of the call was about to come over and distract the player in seat three. Instead, the player in seat three plays a marginal hand that he would have folded and puts a bad beat on you. You take a break to go to the bathroom, and on the way out you walk past the sink because you don't want to take time to wash your hands. You are stuck, and the game is good. You rush back to the table just in time to get a hand. You pick up two Kings, but unfortunately you lose that hand also. You ask the dealer to scramble the cards just before another hand you would otherwise have won, and instead the only thing that gets scrambled is your brain.

The dismal session continues and you forego a party to which you were invited. That's too bad, since you would have met the woman of your dreams and the two of you would have raised a child who would have discovered an anti-virus that would have saved millions of lives. The woman you marry instead, the only one who would put up with your bad run of

Chaos

luck, bears a child whom you have to bail out of jail at age sixteen. You were going to use that money to enter the final event in *The World Series of Poker,* and if the timing was right, you were going to win.

That is all very contrived. But consider the case of a person who wins a tournament. If he had arrived one minute later or earlier and been given a different seat, he probably would not have won. As a matter of fact, if a player at some other table had shown up a minute later or earlier, there may have been a different winner. Without knowing which table he got assigned to, the winner's probability of winning has not changed, and he would likely have won some other tournament if the timing had been different in that case. Using the theory of chaos, we can look in progressively finer detail to see how events came to be. We might find that the winner would have arrived a minute earlier, but he had to stop when a pedestrian entered the crosswalk. Looking closer, that pedestrian was there at that time because he stayed home an extra minute to watch an unusual television commercial. We can examine how that commercial got into that time slot on that station or how the product it advertised came to market, and analyze this situation endlessly.

Are you starting to feel neurotic? Any change in the timing of events may change your future. What should you do to alter these random events that can drastically affect your life? Well, you could take away some of the randomness by always wearing the same clothes, showing up at the same time, parking in the same parking place, sitting in the same chair, … . Just kidding! Of course, you should do nothing. You should concern yourself with things that do make a difference in the probability of success. Don't worry about altering events that won't help you to predict results.

CHAPTER 22

> "If everything seems under control, you're just not going fast enough."
>
> Mario Andretti (1940 -), racecar driver

DIFFERENT LIMITS

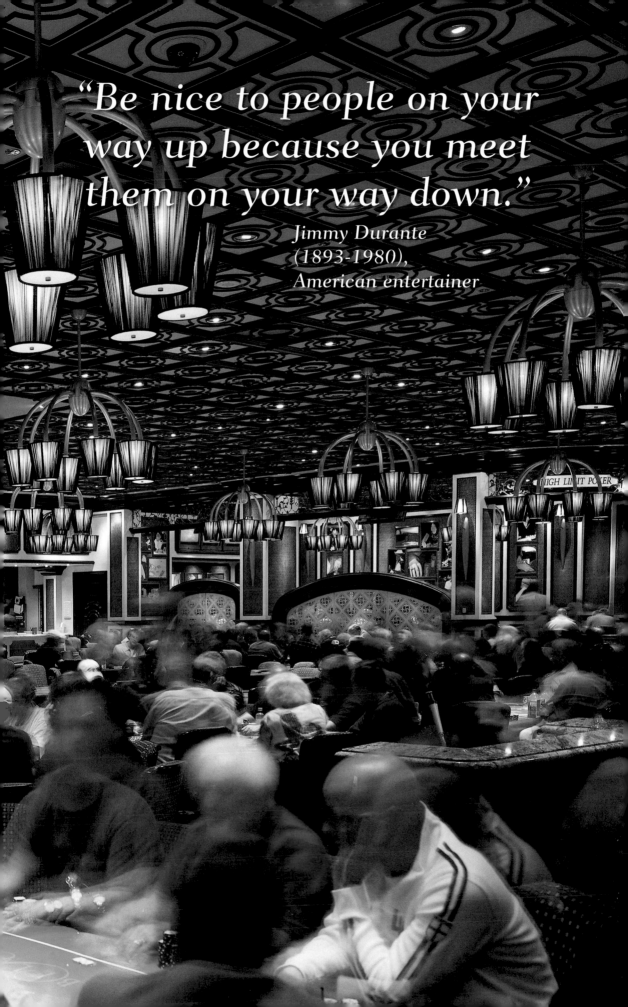

"Be nice to people on your way up because you meet them on your way down."

Jimmy Durante
(1893-1980),
American entertainer

Ace on the River

IN MOST COMPETITIVE ACTIVITIES, THE WORDS *BEGINNER*,
INTERMEDIATE, *ADVANCED*, AND *EXPERT* ARE USED TO DESCRIBE
A PERSON'S LEVEL OF COMPETENCE. **I**N POKER, THE STAKES
FOR WHICH PLAYERS PLAY IS OFTEN USED INSTEAD.

The table below contains my loose definitions of the different stakes
in poker. What I call "Pleasure Poker" may be the rent money to someone
and "Big Limit" may be recreation for a multi-millionaire.

Since the size of a no-limit, pot-limit, or spread-limit game is determined by the money on the table and the action in the game, I have clas-
sified those games by the amount that the big winner will typically win in
a session.

Classification	Limit Poker	No-limit Poker
Pleasure Poker	$4-$8 or less	Big win less than $500
Low Limit	$5-$10 to $20-$40	Big win greater than $500
Middle Limit	$30-$60 to $200-$400	Big win greater than $3000
High Limit	$300-$600 to $800-$1600	Big win greater than $30,000
Big Limit	$1000-$2000 and up	Big win greater than $100,000

Pleasure players are more interested in entertainment than money.

The winning players in low-limit games are the ones who have a reasonable basic strategy for entering the pot. Their awareness of hand values may come from watching the better players in their games, from em-
pirically seeing what works, or from reading.

The winning players in middle-limit games are the ones who have good
betting strategies in later stages of hands. They raise to win extra money
when weak players chase them without getting the right pot odds.

The winning players in high-limit games know how the other players
play and are able to adapt their strategy to exploit the others' weaknesses.
They are also better at recognizing when they are playing badly. They are
very conscious of getting full value on their winning hands and saving bets
on their losing hands.

Winning players in big-limit games are able to play well when they're
losing. They also know how to handle aggressive opponents who seem to
get the last bet in on every street. Many players give up trying to figure

out what aggressive players are doing and resort to checking and calling on every street. Successful big-limit players identify patterns and mannerisms of aggressive players and are able to make informed decisions about whether to raise or fold. In general, they have a more accurate picture of their opponents' hands and don't automatically call on the river in limit poker when it is obvious they have a losing hand. They are not as worried about winning an extra bet as the high-limit players. They try to avoid being tricky when it might cost them the pot, and they make bets or raises that force opponents out of hands. This allows them to win extra pots.

I have defined the limits at which poker is played by using the criterion of the money people gamble for. When I talk about players at a certain level, I actually mean the players who play in open games at those levels and have been successful. A *high-stakes* player is one who plays in high-limit or big-limit games. Using these definitions, wealthy people who gamble with each other in private games would be considered high-stakes players, but not high-limit or big-limit players.

Are there players who have been consistent winners for years in lower and middle-limit games who would win in high-stakes games if they had the bankroll? It is unlikely. It takes a lot of time playing in the higher-limit games to acquire the knowledge necessary to win. High-limit players occasionally mix up the way they play similar hands, and they play each opponent differently. Using a baseball analogy, winning low-limit players are good at handling the slow pitches thrown at them by weak players, but will have trouble with the fastballs, curveballs, and knuckleballs that they have to face in the higher-limit games.

CHAPTER 23

"He is the greatest money manager in the world. He always manages to come up with money."

David Heyden (1950-) about poker player, cardroom manager, and chronic overspender Eric Drache (1943-)

MONEY MANAGEMENT

"I'm living so far beyond my income that we may almost be said to be living apart."

e. e. cummings
(1894-1962),
American poet

WHAT AMOUNT SHOULD YOU BUY IN WITH?
HOW CAN YOU MINIMIZE YOUR LOSSES?

How much money should you buy in with when you play poker? I usually buy in for the minimum, although some players like to have a lot of chips on the table at all times. Here are some considerations to help you determine how much you should start with.

REASONS FOR A MINIMUM BUY-IN

1. There is a mathematical edge when you have fewer chips than are needed to call all bets, since you can't be driven out of a hand when you are all-in. This is especially powerful In no-limit and pot limit, where it is much easier to play a short stack.

2. It gives you a low profile, so people won't ask you to lend, stake, or invest as frequently.

3. You will not be targeted as a big winner, so others won't be afraid to play with you.

4. It is easier to limit losses.

5. When your stack is so short that you don't have enough money to play a hand out, you won't start with a weak hand with the intention of bluffing at a time when people are more likely to call you.

6. You have a better chance of keeping hit-and-run artists at the table, because they can't get as far ahead when you have less for them to win.

7. You probably play better when you are ahead and worse when you are stuck. Even if you won't admit that, you would agree that your opponents play better when *they* are ahead and worse when *they* are stuck. Therefore, you will have money in front of you when you should, and be short of money when your opponents are at their best.

8. If you are on a short bankroll, you must protect yourself from going broke. For example, three $200 buy-ins will protect you better than one $600 buy-in.

REASONS FOR A LARGE BUY-IN

1. If you are one of the best players, you want to have maximum play on hands. You use your chips as a tool for making better plays than your opponents.

2. Opponents would rather play with you if they think they can win a lot.

3. Gamblers don't like playing with someone who appears nitty.

4. When the game is especially good, there is a race between the better players to get the loose money that is being thrown around. You need enough chips to be able to get your share.

5. You make it more difficult for people to know when you are losing.

6. You may feel more confident with a lot of chips in front of you.

7. You can avoid having to make the play adjustments that are necessary when playing a short stack. You can play drawing hands profitably when there is a lot to gain.

Many players keep records of their poker sessions and do some kind of statistical analysis on the data. Calculation of different statistical quantities and discussions about the number of bets you need for a game are not very useful. Most players initiate record keeping after a win since it is more satisfying to start with a win than a loss. You should keep records for tax reasons, and also so you can examine how you have done in various gambling endeavors. These records may help you determine the stakes and games you should play in. When you need to make money, you should play in a game in which you have been a consistent winner. If that game doesn't exist for you at any level, then you must be very selective when you are short of money. If that doesn't work, you probably need to find a job to fund your poker habit.

A player who is losing a lot, especially in a limit game, shouldn't focus on trying to get even. Instead, he should think about getting some of his money back. Losing $3000 in an $80-$160 game after being stuck $6000 is a good comeback.

Is it wrong to keep playing in a game when you are stuck, if you would have quit the game if you were ahead? Most experts will tell you it's one long game, so you should evaluate each situation independently of how you are doing. This is not necessarily correct. You can continue, as long as playing a lengthy session will not cause you to miss a better game the next day. If I am losing but playing reasonably well and have an edge, I usually stay in the game. I think of it as working overtime, which I don't always have the drive and adrenaline to do. On the other hand, if I am winning but only have a 1% edge, I might decide to quit so I could do something enjoyable.

Smart players congratulate themselves whenever they quit a game in which they are losing. When I quit because the game is not very good or because I have been playing poorly, I may give myself a pep talk that sounds like this:

"This is what distinguishes me from other players, because very few can make this kind of decision. I'm going to enjoy a good meal and watch a movie. I'm aggravated by the loss, but I'm not going to let those jerks control me. When I'm ahead and they're stuck, they won't be able to quit, and then I will get my revenge."

Chapter 24

Poker
on the
Internet

"It would appear that we have reached the limits of what it is possible to achieve with computer technology, although one should be careful with such statements, as they tend to sound pretty silly in five years."

John von Neumann
(1903-1957),
Hungarian-born American
mathematician and pioneer in
computers and game theory

Ace on the River

ONLINE POKER HAS BECOME THE STARTING GROUND FOR MOST YOUNG PLAYERS.

It should not be surprising to see many unknown tournament winners over the next few years, since these apparently inexperienced players will have played many hours in online tournaments. Beginners can play for play money or for as little as 1 cent – 2 cents. There are freeroll tournaments every day on the Internet. Some are worthwhile, but most are not. Some sites have freeroll tournaments that pay thousands of dollars, while others require you to beat 2000 entrants to win less than $100.

When playing in online games or tournaments, it may be helpful to record the names of players and make notes on their play. Some poker-site providers have a "Notes" option to facilitate this. In a live game, you can easily connect faces to players. Some providers allow you the option of supplying a picture for your personal icon. If you are playing for entertainment, you may do this if you wish, but if you are playing for serious money, don't make it easier for your opponents to remember you. Also, you should change your screen name periodically if you think opponents with whom you frequently play have adapted to your style.

When playing in a live game, you get a lot of information from the tempo of your opponents' play, the way they put their chips into the pot (in small stacks, in large stacks, spraying chips, forceful movements), their facial expressions, their grabbing of chips before it is their turn, the intonation of their spoken bets and raises, and their conversation while in a hand. Proper hand selection is more important when playing online, because you won't be able to use your people-reading skills as you can in live games. But there are online tells that you can take advantage of. Some players use the bet/raise buttons when they have a good hand, so their bets and raises happen immediately when it is their turn. They may get into a rhythm that gives away valuable

Poker on the Internet

information, especially when playing heads-up where it is more notice-able.

I don't believe anyone can become a top player solely by playing on the Internet. A person's mannerisms and body language, which can be observed in a live game, often reveal important information about his thought processes. Also, the discussions about a hand after it is over may provide instructive ideas. Even if you disagree with an opinion that is expressed, you will still gain valuable insights which will help you against players whose methods differ from yours.

In a live game, you win many pots where you are the first to show your hand and your opponent mucks his hand. You might like to know your opponent's hand, so you can learn more about his style of play, but asking to see the losing hand is usually considered a breach of etiquette. When you play poker online, you can check the "Hand Histories" that are provided. Players often use them after a session is over to evaluate their own play and check for possible collusion between others. The most valuable time to get a hand history is when your opponent has called to the river and lost, but his hand wasn't shown. This is especially important when you are playing someone heads-up.

I recommend using the Internet to practice playing forms of poker in which one is weak. But most players are there to make money, not to practice. Limit hold'em will usually be the Internet player's game of choice because it is the easiest game to play on autopilot. People playing at home are often multitasking, including playing multiple sessions of Internet poker at the same time.

The ease with which one can play poker online makes it very addictive. You can wake up, get on your computer, and play in the privacy of your own room. Many professional poker players spend the entire day in their underwear and bathrobes (only a slight downgrade from their live-game attire) while playing poker on their computers.

Ace on the River

On the Internet, at least twice as many hands are played in the same length of time, so you will see more strange things happen than usual. For example, you will see more than twice as many draw-outs because there is much more chasing, since it takes minimal effort to click on the "call" or "raise" button and it is much easier to steam when no one knows who you are.

Although the game proceeds at a faster pace, there is not enough sensory input when you are out of a hand. Consequently, you may want to play two games at a time to help you avoid playing too many hands out of boredom. Even a middle-limit player is probably better off playing two $10-$20 games rather than one $20-$40 game. It is easy to play multiple games because you can act ahead of your turn without anyone knowing about it. Also, you are prompted when it is your turn to play, so you don't have to be as attentive as in a live game.

Playing more than two games at a time may increase your winnings, but it can result in more misclicks and misplays, which will lower your percentage advantage. It is easy to get into a rut where you call all the time on the river no matter how remote your chance of winning. It's like driving for a long time and getting hypnotized by the road. If you play multiple games for long periods of time, you should take frequent breaks so you can continue to stay alert.

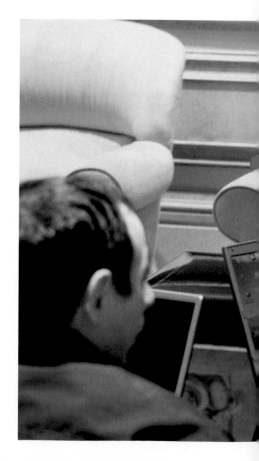

Collusion is a possibility, as was mentioned in the *Protecting Yourself* chapter. If you think you are being cheated, do as you would in a normal cardroom. If you are winning enough to make it worth your time, keep playing. If you continually lose, quit.

Sophisticated Internet players have high-resolution screens which comfortably allow four games to be played at the same time. A motivated high-stakes player should have accounts at all the reputable poker sites so he can play in two to four games at the same time, averaging around $150-$300 limit for his total action. Playing fifty hours per week, four weeks per month, while maintaining a 1% advantage, yields:

$300 x 1/3 (big bet per hour)
x 2 (twice as many hands)
x 200 (hours per month)
= $40,000 per month.

This calculation above uses the assumption that a 3% advantage is approximately equal to a win of one big bet per hour, as was discussed in the *Making Money* chapter. Based on this assumption, I substituted 1/3 big bet per hour for a 1% advantage, on the left-hand side of the equation.

Those few players who are willing to put in the time and are able to maintain greater than a 2% advantage can make more than a million dollars in a year. However, most players who are capable of doing that would have a better chance in live games, where it is possible to make that kind of money without getting burned out in the process.

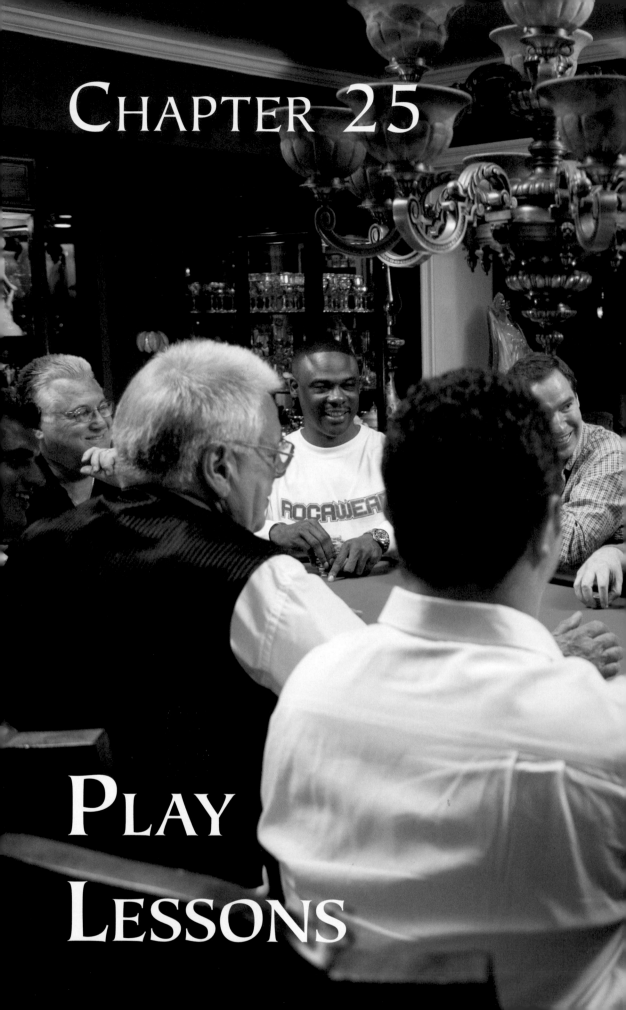

CHAPTER 25

PLAY LESSONS

"I am enough of an artist to draw freely upon my imagination. Imagination is more important than knowledge. Knowledge is limited. Imagination encircles the world."

Albert Einstein
(1879-1955),
physicist

"I have not failed. I've just found 10,000 ways that won't work."

Thomas Alva Edison
(1847-1931),
American inventor

Ace on the River

A COMPLETE PLAYER INCORPORATES A VARIETY OF CONCEPTS TAKEN FROM DIFFERENT FORMS OF POKER.

An experienced player will use knowledge acquired from playing and reading to formulate a basic strategy for starting hands. He will have a memorized basic strategy of which hands to play in the various positions (early, middle, late, and blinds) in hold'em and lowball.

In Omaha games, there are too many possible starting hands to memorize. In stud games, the upcards of the opponents create too many possibilities to memorize all situations. In Omaha and stud, you should have general ideas of which hands to play.

Once you have settled on a consistent set of starting hands, you will occasionally deviate from them as a counter to your opponents' strategies. More adjustments to your starting hand play are required when someone enters the pot ahead of you. Even on the first betting round, you will face continual borderline decisions where you may fold, call, or raise.

Play Lessons

LESSON 1: YOU OFTEN PLAY THE SAME HAND DIFFERENTLY AGAINST DIFFERENT OPPONENTS OR UNDER DIFFERENT CIRCUMSTANCES.

Example 1a: Limit hold'em.

You have K♣ Q♥ in late position, with a raise ahead of you by a player in middle position. Against a tight player, it is probably correct to fold. Against a slightly looser-than-average player, it may be right to call. Against a wild player, it is probably right to reraise to try to isolate him.

Even against average players, your options may be to reraise or fold. You reraise if you think they think you are playing tight. You fold if you think they think you are playing loose and you anticipate that they will call you down with an underpair.

In seven-card stud, every time someone raises on the first three cards with a card higher than your pair and you are behind the raiser, you have to decide whether to fold, call, or raise.

Example 1b: Seven-card stud.

The low card brings it in, two players fold, a player with an Eight up raises, another folds, and now it's your turn. You start out with a pair of Fives and a King kicker.

If one Five or two Kings are out, you should fold as part of your basic strategy. If there are two or more unpaired cards higher than an Eight behind you, then you give the raiser credit for a better hand, which tempts you to fold. If one of the Fives is the same suit as the King, this is a small factor influencing you to call. If the upcards behind you are small, this sways you towards calling or reraising, because there is a greater chance that the initial raiser was trying to steal. You will generally fold against a solid player, and often call or reraise against a loose player. If the King was your upcard instead of one of the Fives, you would be inclined to reraise instead of calling or folding.

As the play continues to other betting streets, you will be faced with a lot of information, and you will have to quickly decide whether to check, fold, call, or raise. You must consider all the ways a hand can be played and analyze which would be the best.

Every play has a context. I may have identical hands in what may seem like identical situations to a lesser player, but I will take different courses of action. Body language is incorporated into my decision. Based on the

Ace on the River

past, or based even more on the last few minutes, I will try to determine what this opponent is doing, what he will think I have, and what his response to my action will be. Considering his actions, what is the range of hands he would play that way? What is the most likely hand that I expect him to have? How will the play I am going to make set him up for something I will do in the future? Should I check and call on this street instead of betting, to misrepresent the strength of my hand? If I bet here, will I be called only when I am beat? Should I fold my marginal hand because this opponent never bluffs in this particular situation? For example, he never bluffs by raising on the river. You will be unable to ask and answer all those questions in real time, but as you gain experience, you will automatically know which questions are relevant in a given situation.

You can't become an expert player unless you are able to determine the perfect way and the correct way to play most hands after seeing your opponents' cards when the hand is over.

Perfect Play: The play that would have been made at each stage of a hand if the opponents' hole cards had been known.

Correct Play: Given the information available at the time, the play that yields the best average result.

When you get to see your opponent's cards at the end of the hand, which often occurs when his winning hand is shown, the *perfect play* will usually be clear. If you don't get to see your opponents' cards, you may not be able to make this kind of analysis. However, you might be able to make an educated guess about what his hand was by taking into account what happened on prior betting rounds. Analyzing hands after they are over will allow you to make better decisions the next time a similar situation arises.

Play Lessons

LESSON 2: IF YOU HAVE A GOOD HAND, IT IS USUALLY PREFERABLE TO BET THAN TO CHECK TO SET A TRAP.

You will usually check if you have to act before the player who has the betting lead, even when you have a very good hand. This is not the trapping play that is being criticized here. When you have the betting lead, or when the player with the betting lead checks to you, it is usually correct to bet, to build the pot and to prevent opponents from drawing out.

Example 2: Limit hold'em.

You have A♥ K♣. A player limps in middle position, and you raise on the button. Everyone folds except the limper. The flop comes:

The opponent checks. You decide to check to try to trap him.

The turn card is the 5♦. He bets, you raise, he reraises, and you call.

The river card is the 8♣. He bets. You call. He shows 5♠ 5♥.

Now you realize the *perfect play* would have been to bet on the flop. You would probably not have made any more money on the hand no matter what card came, but you could lose some. Don't base your analysis solely on results and conclude that a check would have been the *perfect play* if a Five didn't come. *Perfect play* uses knowledge of your opponents' cards, not future board cards.

If you analyze the hand further, you realize that when your opponent has an Ace or possibly even a Ten, you will get action, and maybe more action overall than if you check on the flop. You should conclude that the *correct play* is to bet your hand on the flop.

Ace on the River

LESSON 3: IF YOU DON'T HAVE A VERY GOOD HAND OR DRAW, FOLD AT THE EARLIEST OPPORTUNITY.

Example 3: Limit hold'em.

You hold 9♦ 7♦. A player raises in late position. Everyone folds to you, and you call in the big blind. The flop is

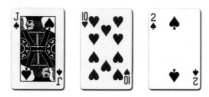

Your opponent bets and you call, hoping to make a straight. The 3♦ comes on the turn. You check and your opponent checks. The K♣ comes on the river. You and your opponent both check again. He turns over A♥ 6♥. The *perfect play* would have been to check-raise on the flop and bet on the turn if he had called on the flop, because he probably would have folded.

Even if you had made a straight on the turn, it wouldn't have been the nuts, and in some cases your opponent may have had redraws at a flush or a higher straight, not to mention a full house. Drawing to undercards with a gut-shot is not usually a profitable play. Drawing to the undercard gut-shot when your opponent may have a flush draw is really asking for trouble. The *correct play* was folding on the flop, although that differs from the *perfect play*.

There are many times that you could win on the flop by check-raising, but you are trying to tailor your play to the maximum number of hands your opponent may have. Similarly, many times you will bet with nothing, only to lose a bet you didn't have to, because you would rather make a mistake that costs you a bet than make a mistake that costs you the pot. Of course, if your opponent makes a suspicious check, you want to avoid betting and getting check-raised out of a pot you might have won if you had hit a perfect card.

Play Lessons

LESSON 4: RECOGNIZE SCARE CARDS THAT MAY ALLOW YOU TO BLUFF YOUR OPPONENTS.

Example 4: No-limit hold'em, $25 and $50 blinds.

You open for $150 in middle position with Q♠ J♠ and get called by an opponent in late position. The flop is

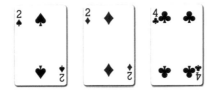

You bet $300 on the flop and are called. Your only hope seems to be a Queen or Jack on the turn, but the turn is the A♥. You check and your opponent checks. The river is the 10♥. You check and your opponent shows two Eights.

You were so preoccupied with hoping to catch a good card that you failed to recognize a good opportunity. When the Ace came on the turn, you should have made the *perfect play* of betting about $800. If your opponent had a medium pair, as you may have suspected, the good turn cards were not only a Queen or a Jack, but also an Ace or a King.

When you catch a card on the turn that improves your hand, you still have to decide how to bet, as shown in the next lesson.

Ace on the River

LESSON 5: **IF YOUR BETS DEFINE THE STRENGTH OF YOUR HAND, IT MAY MAKE DECISIONS EASIER FOR YOU ON LATER STREETS.**

Example 5: No-limit hold'em, $25-$50 blinds.

You open for $150 in late position with K♣ Q♣ and get called by the opponent in the big blind. The flop is

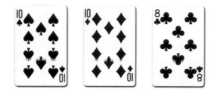

After your opponent checks, you bet $300 hoping to steal the pot, but he calls. You suspect that he has three Tens and is hoping that you will make another bet on the turn. You are pleasantly surprised when the K♥ comes on the turn, but you wonder if this card is only going to cause you to lose more money in the event that he has three Tens. You come up with a solution that may help you avoid his trap. If you check, he can't raise you out of the pot, and your tricky play may induce a bluff from him on the river in some cases. If he bets on the river you will call, figuring that if he has trips you will lose the same amount of money as if you had bet on the turn. If he checks on the river you will probably bet, since it is unlikely he would check trips at this point.

The 7♣ comes on the river, your opponent bets $600, and you call. He shows you J♦ 9♦, which gives him a straight.

You gave him a free card and got burned. On the turn, the *perfect play* would have been a bet that is approximately the size of the pot. He would probably have folded. But what if he had three Tens? You were likely to lose money any way you played it. You should have made a large enough bet on the turn to represent a certain minimum strength of your hand to your opponent. That is, you should *define your hand* so that you can accurately interpret the subsequent actions of your opponent. Then, if you are raised on the turn, you can fold with confidence, knowing that you are beat.

Play Lessons

Lesson 6: Evaluate if there is more to gain from bluffing than trying to win only when you make your hand.

Example 6a: Triple-draw lowball. (I constructed an example that works in either Ace-to-Five or Deuce-to-Seven.)

One player raises, you call in the small blind with 2 3 6 6 K, and the big blind calls. The draw is two cards by you, three cards by the big blind, and two cards by the raiser. You catch a Three and a Ten, and check. The big blind checks. The original raiser bets, and you and the big blind call. Everybody draws two on the second round. You catch a Six and a Queen. You check and the others check behind you. Everybody draws two.

If you draw and hit high cards, you will wish you had stood pat. Standing pat and betting was probably the *correct play*, especially if your opponents frequently fold when they miss in this situation. If they've seen you make this kind of play before, and the original raiser will almost surely pay you off, then you should draw.

What would opponents you play with have done in your situation? When playing triple-draw, you should have a good idea of the frequency with which each of your opponents is likely to stay pat on the third draw and bluff, so you know what to do when the play we just discussed is made against you.

I will use seven-card stud for several examples, because it is a very useful game for the purpose of poker discussion. With the many possibilities of initial upcards, even starting situations have great variability. With new information provided on every street, there is a lot of data that needs to be processed in order to play seven-card stud well.

Example 6b: Seven-card stud.

You are the bring-in with the 2♣ up and another Deuce and a King in the hole. A player with the A♣ up in late position raises, and you call. You call a bet on fourth street and he bets again on fifth street with the boards as follows:

You

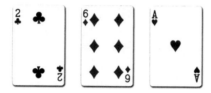

Your hole cards

Opponent

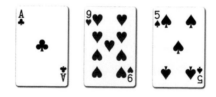

If he was originally stealing and hasn't improved, you could take this pot away from him with a raise. If he had a big pair to start, you would be better off folding. When it is right either to fold or raise, many players call as a compromise. It is usually better to take a course of action that can be right. On this hand, you should raise against a player who will keep betting in this situation on a steal. If you get reraised, fold.

If you raise here, you feel as if you are bluffing, although you might actually have the best hand. If you get called, you might improve on the next two cards and end up with the best hand. This type of bluff is called a semi-bluff, since you might win if your opponent folds the best hand or if you complete your draw.

In hold'em, I like to semi-bluff on the turn when I have a draw. If I raise with cards that are related to the board, there is a chance that my opponent will fold immediately, or he will have fewer outs that would allow him to call my subsequent bet on the river because my hand contains cards he needs.

Example 6c: Limit hold'em.

You have 7♥ 6♥ in the big blind. You call a raise and the flop is

The turn is the K♦.

Against an opponent who will continue betting regardless of whether he has a pair or not, I will call on the flop and check-raise on the turn. Similarly, if I had flopped a flush draw I may have waited until the turn to check-raise. This tactic will allow me to win pots in which my opponent also has a draw and we both miss. Players are accustomed to being raised on the flop with a draw or for the purpose of getting a free card on the turn, but they normally envision that they are up against a stronger hand when the raise comes on a later street. Also, the earlier raise will be less effective if my opponent decides to reraise on the flop with only overcards in his hand, in an effort to see the turn and river without putting more money in the pot. This can thwart my ability to win the pot without making a hand.

In cases where I am up against more than one opponent, I just call on the flop. In limit poker, it is usually too risky to attempt a bluff against more than one opponent. I try to make a profit as a result of the extra pot odds I am getting.

Ace on the River

Example 6d: Seven-card stud.

The 3♠ brings it in and you raise in early position with the 10♣ up and J♣ 9♣ in the hole. You are reraised in middle position by a good player who has the 5♦ up. Everyone else folds and you decide to put in a third bet.

The boards end up:

You

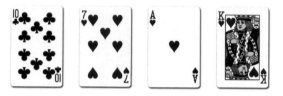

Your hole cards

Good player

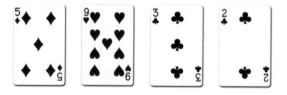

196

Play Lessons

You bet all the way, and on sixth street you bet and are raised. What is going on? Surely the Deuce didn't help him. Could he have A♦ 4♦ or 6♦ 4♦ in the hole? He probably would not have reraised initially with those holdings. Could he have been rolled up? He probably would have played differently on third street and fifth street. You know you are going to call, but you pause to decide whether you are going to bet out or try for a check-raise if you make a straight on the river. You call after deciding you are going to check if you make the straight. You catch a Ten on the river and check with your pair of Tens. Your opponent also checks and shows you two Kings out of the hole, the hand he represented at the start.

Now you realize that betting out on the river if you had made a straight would have been a better plan. Then you come to the conclusion that if you had reraised on sixth street, the *perfect play*, he would have been hard pressed to call. It probably would have been worth the gamble.

LESSON 7: ON LATER STREETS, VISUALIZE YOUR OPPONENTS' POSSIBLE HANDS AND BET IN ACCORDANCE WITH LOGICAL POSSIBILITIES.

Example 7a: Seven-card stud.

A Deuce brought it in, the next two players folded, the J♦ raised, and you reraised with the Q♣ up and a Queen and a Six in the hole. All folded except the original raiser, a winning high-stakes player, who called. There were no Jacks or Queens out. One other diamond and one other club were out. There was an overcard to your left, an Ace.

After six cards, the boards look like this:

Opponent

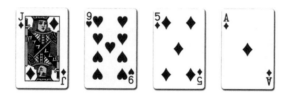

You

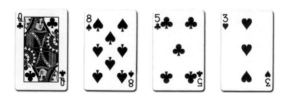

Your hole cards

You bet and were called on fourth and fifth street. You make the "negative inference" that your opponent doesn't have a flush draw, since this opponent frequently raises on fifth street with a flush draw, although he may have been deterred by the two clubs you have in your board. You suspect that he has an Ace or King kicker in the hole, because otherwise he might have folded at this point. He might already have two pair and may have been waiting to raise on sixth street if you didn't catch another club or an open pair. He may have been calling because of the additional two-card outs he had with three to a flush or three to a straight. Or he may just want to chase this one down with two Jacks.

He checks to you on sixth street. If you bet, he obviously won't fold even if he only has split Jacks since your board is not intimidating. If you bet and he has made the flush or Aces up, he will raise. You bet anyway because you have to make him pay to draw, and there is a chance he would have bet into you if the A♦ had helped him. You breathe a sigh of relief when he only calls. He checks on the river, and you catch a Five. You bet your Queens up, hoping he will call with Jacks up or only Jacks, but instead he check-raises.

What a sickening development! You wish you had your bet back. Before you bet on the river, you should have considered whether this is an opponent who usually would have bet out on the river with Jacks up, but normally would have checked for a check-raise with better hands. You showed strength when you bet against his board on sixth street. It is unlikely that you would have been called if he ended up with only one pair. You decide to fold, but you probably shouldn't have bet in the first place.

What would you have done if this opponent had bet into you on the river, representing Jacks up? Answer: Against most good players, you should raise without even looking at your last card. However, against very predictable opponents, you make plays that exploit their weaknesses. If this opponent will usually fold to a raise with Jacks up but call with better hands, then you might as well look, and raise when your hand *doesn't* improve and you end up with only Queens. If he would almost always check with worse than two pair, and he will normally call a raise here, then you should fold if you don't improve.

Example 7b: Seven-card stud.

The 4♦ brings it in. A player with the 5♥ raises and you double raise with the Q♦ upcard and the Q♠ 7♠ in the hole. A strong player to your left calls two bets with the 8♦ up. The original raiser, a weak predictable player, reraises. It seems obvious he has two Aces or two Kings in the hole. You make open Queens on fourth street. You bet and maintain the betting lead the rest of the way. Both opponents call you to the river, and the boards read as follows.

Weak Player

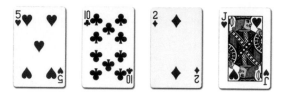

You

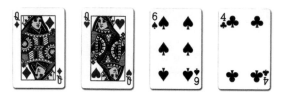

Your hole cards

Strong Player

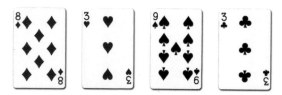

The strong player must have been rolled up. You fill up with the 7♦ on the river. You bet, hoping that someone will improve. The strong player hesitates and calls, and the weak player raises. He must have made big trips, so you quickly reraise and both opponents call.

Play Lessons

You show your hand, and the strong player shows you he had Eights full as he slides his hand into the muck. You knew when he called the reraise he had to have more than trips, since he knew the weak player had big trips. Now you think, "Why didn't he initially raise you on the river?" He must have figured he could get the same money if he got an overcall by the weak player, without risking a reraise from you. Piecing this together, you start to see what the *perfect play* was, and it might very well have been the *correct play*. You could have just called the raise by the weak player on the river, representing only trip Queens. You may get an overcall from three Eights, but you will hit the jackpot when he has Eights full. He will now reraise, and when it comes back to you, you confound them both with the fourth bet.

There are situations where your opponent is always going to bet when your hand is beat, but will check when you have the best hand. It is usually best to bet on the river on these occasions when you are first to act. (This is a *value-bet*.) This frequently happens in seven-card stud when you make two small pair on the river and your opponent would bet with two bigger pair but check with one big pair.

Ace on the River

Example 7c: Limit hold'em.

You have A♥ 2♥ in the small blind. A player raises and you are the only caller. The flop is

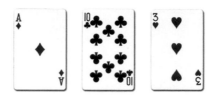

You check, he bets, and you check-raise. The 5♠ comes on the turn, and you bet and get called. The 9♣ comes on the river. You think he has an Ace with a bigger kicker. You should make a value-bet even though you think you are beat, since you are going to call if he bets and you don't want to save him a bet if he has a Ten or a pocket pair of Jacks, Queens, or Kings.

In many of the previous examples a mistake was made. You will do most of your thinking about hands that you lost. There will be hands where you play badly and win, and you learn a lesson from them because you realize how lucky you needed to get to win the pot. But the lessons you learn from those hands will not stay with you as long as the lessons you learn from hands you lose.

You may not agree with the analyses in the examples, or you might not think enough information was given. These examples serve to show some of the thought processes required to become a better player. Approaching poker hands in this way will increase your ability to consider all the possibilities in real time as you play.

On several hands, an aggressive bluffing course of action was suggested. You should play according to what you think is going on. Players often say, "I knew he was weak. I could have raised." If you know your opponent is weak and can't stand a raise, then raise. You may think that the opponents can counter this by calling you down whenever you play aggressively. The beauty of being aggressive is that it allows you to play your good hands strongly. You will get a lot of action from opponents with substandard hands when they misread you for a bluff.

Good players do most of their thinking after losing sessions. Bad players want to block losing sessions out of their mind. Think about hands

Play Lessons

you lost and see if you could have played them differently with a better result. Always think about what actions you would have taken if you had known what your opponents' hands actually were. Then try to recall if there were any hints available that would tell you about their hands.

Some players who criticize themselves are too results-oriented. They chastise themselves for not raising in stud if the raise would have knocked someone out, enabling them to catch a more beneficial card. They think it was right to have called if they would have ended up making their draw, and it was wrong to call whenever they miss. There are many hands you will play correctly and lose, although you may later decide, especially in a three-way pot, that you should have check-raised and knocked out the hand that beat you.

Notice how players bet. Who shows weakness with strong hands and strength with weak hands? What are their talking patterns with strong and weak hands? How do they act when they catch a card that helps their hand? What kind of playing tempo do they have with strong and weak hands? Know which players to your left act as if they are folding when they have a strong hand. Make this assessment before it is your turn to play, since it is unethical to hesitate to get players to act out of turn.

Many plays are neither right nor wrong, but are just different ways to play a hand. These differences in the play of similar hands will keep opponents off balance. A play that looks bad or doesn't work on one hand may generate a mistake from an opponent on another. Players who make their opponents play badly often don't get the credit they deserve. The "starting-hand policemen" say, "Look what he started with!" There are players who appear to play more hands than they should, but win because they bet their hands well and force their opponents to guess what they are doing.

These loose players may make mathematically incorrect plays on one hand which will affect their opponents' play on future hands. Another situation in which I may make a mathematically incorrect play is when I take a stand by calling or raising an overly aggressive opponent to prevent him from running over me. I have also made an extremely "bad" call against a live one when I knew he would quit if he won the pot, but might stay and lose a lot if I drew out on him. I hate to admit it, but on rare occasions I have made a terrible call when I was steaming, with the hope that I would win the pot and get back on my feet. However, I don't recommend this last tactic.

Ace on the River

Most players know they have to adjust to their opponents' styles, but they often make the wrong adjustments. An old poker adage is: "Play tight in a loose game and play loose in a tight game." This may work in low-limit poker, but against experienced players it doesn't take into account that your opponents will make adjustments to your style also. Good players will give action to loose players, but they will only play against a tight player with hands that meet higher standards.

LESSON 8. SOME OPPONENTS WILL PRESSURE YOU INTO MAKING MISTAKES. ADJUST YOUR PLAY TO COUNTERACT THEIR STRATEGY.

Here are examples of styles of play and adjustments:

Opponent's Tactic	Typical Incorrect Adjustment	Better Adjustment
Extremely loose play	Wait for a good hand.	Loosen your standards and reraise frequently.
Excessive value-betting	Call with almost anything.	Raise when you can beat a value-bet; raise-bluff more often on the river.
Frequent check-raising	Give too many free cards.	Bet normally, except when you want a free card and are confident you will be check-raised.
Antagonizing opponents	Get emotionally involved; focus on beating the culprit and showing him up.	Ignore him and try to play well.

Trying to make great plays against a weak player is usually not a good idea because a weak player will not respond the way an expert would. It is sometimes likened to playing Beethoven to a cow. Players who try this will say, "He should have known what I represented by the way I played the hand, and he should never have called me." You normally beat weak players by playing better hands and allowing them to play badly against you. Over a long period of time, the better players will adjust to their opponents' play, luck will even out, and weakness in strategy will be exposed.

I typically make more than twenty plays in a session that in retrospect I think were mistakes. Some are clear blunders that cost me the pot or

Play Lessons

caused me to lose more money than I should have on a hand. Others are more subtle. Maybe I should have check-called or check-raised instead of beting. Sometimes I should have folded instead of calling, or called or raised instead of folding. Yet, I have played with people who have told me they play almost flawlessly. I have never respected the play of anyone who has said that. I think they mean that every hand they played and every bet they made would have gotten the Good Housekeeping Seal of Approval from the starting-hand policemen, since their hands were solid for the particular bet or call they made. On the other hand, I'm capable of raising or calling with any hand with the intention of betting or raising later, when I think that will enable me to win the pot.

I believe the game of poker is so complex that we all make many bad decisions, but the best players win by making fewer than others. It reminds me of what Lee Trevino said when he was asked if he chokes. He admitted, "Of course I choke, but I look around and see other players choking worse than I do. That's why I'm able to win golf tournaments."

CHAPTER 26

TOURNAMENTS

"Victory goes to the player who makes the next-to-last mistake."

Savielly Grigorievitch Tartakower
(1887-1956),
Ukrainian chess master

Ace on the River

TOURNAMENT RESULTS ARE THE PUBLIC MEASURE OF A PLAYER'S SUCCESS.

Poker tournaments are like lotteries, but with much better odds and an element of skill thrown in. Entering a tournament follows the sound principle of getting into a situation where a player can win a lot more than he can lose. Players invest a fixed amount except in rebuy tournaments. There is no hustling of unwitting opponents into losing more than they planned, which is one of the negative aspects associated with gambling. Media coverage focuses on the competitive angle, and it puts poker on a level with other sports as entertainment for the viewing public.

In a tournament, as players attempt to accumulate chips, the stakes keep increasing. A tournament is like a time-lapse photography view of a poker career, where the players move up to a higher limit approximately every hour. They can't sit and wait for premium hands, since their chip amount is effectively cut in half every time the limits double. Those with volatile styles who build up chips quickly or lose them quickly are naturals for tournaments.

A winning high-stakes side-game player will not be impressed with the play of the average tournament player. In sports, the competitors need credentials to qualify. All that is required to enter a poker tournament is money. The luck factor in poker, which is increased by the rapid raising of stakes, gives almost every player in the field a chance to

Tournaments

do well in a tournament. Players, who in past years were the catalysts for side games, are now using their money to pay for tournament and satellite buy-ins.

Why don't all of the best players play in tournaments on a regular basis? Some don't enter them because the results are reported to the IRS, and they don't want to pay full taxes on their winnings. Also, many high-stakes players conclude that if they have a good run of luck in the side games, they will make more money than they would have in the tournament. If they hang on for several hours in the tournament and finish out of the money or in one of the lower paying places, they will have lost a day of work.

Some players go to several stops on the tournament circuit with the sole intent of playing in the accompanying side games, which tend to be much more lucrative during tournaments. There is great value in playing side games with seats available for emotionally drained players who just got knocked out of the daily event at a tournament. Don't be one of the victims. If you last a long time in a tournament, don't play in a side game immediately after getting knocked out. Tournament play is more tiring than side-game play.

If there were no extrinsic value to winning tournaments, they probably would not be worth the time. Some extrinsic benefits of tournaments are the accomplishment of a well-defined goal, getting one's name in a tournament write-up for family and friends to see, television coverage in the bigger events, and the respect or envy of one's peers. Another value that is often overlooked is just the fun of competing in tournaments. However, many players don't view tournaments as fun, because all entrants except the winner go broke on their last hand and end up with something to feel badly about. Although getting knocked out is very aggravating, winning is a lot of fun.

Some professional tournament players get extra value by using other people's money. They may sell pieces of themselves at a premium. For example, they sell 10% of themselves for 15% to 20% of the buy-in to a few different people. Many get completely staked because they can't make enough money to support themselves. These players are experts in self-promotion. They need to attract investors who will help defray the costs of tournaments, including travel, hotel expenses, and the ever-increasing tournament entry fees tacked onto the cost of the buy-ins. If their make-up figures get too large, the staked players turn to other backers, so there are profits to split up when they win.

If a professional tournament player exhibits extreme emotion when he is knocked out, one should remember that this is his livelihood because he may not be able to beat the side games. In tournaments it's boom or bust. When he hits, he may overspend and will not be prepared for the inevitable long dry spell.

Some tournament players swap pieces with other players. This gives them an extra rooting interest and they figure it helps to even out the luck factor, so they won't have to wait as long between cashouts. If the pieces swapped are less than 5%, there is probably no harm, but anything more than that could be an incentive for collusion, as was mentioned in the *Protecting Yourself* section.

When I played in my first poker tournament, the final event of the 1991 *World Series of Poker*, an experienced tournament player asked me if I would swap 3% with him. I acknowledged that he certainly knew more about playing tournaments than I did, but I told him I never take a piece of anyone and I have never had anyone take a piece of me. He got upset and asked Erik Seidel, a very successful tournament player, to explain how insulting my refusal was. He knew I respected Erik, who had been a big winner in side games before he started focusing his attention on tournaments. Erik explained that many good play-

Tournaments

ers swap small pieces with several players in a tournament to even out the luck factor. I asked him if he had made money doing this. He told me, "I have done pretty well in tournaments, so I guess swapping has cost me a few hundred thousand dollars."

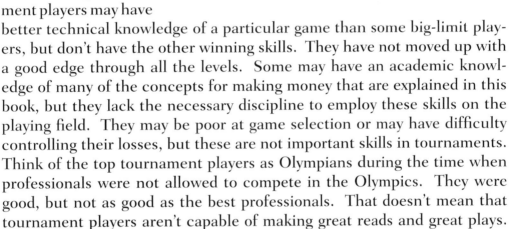

Some top tournament players may have better technical knowledge of a particular game than some big-limit players, but don't have the other winning skills. They have not moved up with a good edge through all the levels. Some may have an academic knowledge of many of the concepts for making money that are explained in this book, but they lack the necessary discipline to employ these skills on the playing field. They may be poor at game selection or may have difficulty controlling their losses, but these are not important skills in tournaments. Think of the top tournament players as Olympians during the time when professionals were not allowed to compete in the Olympics. They were good, but not as good as the best professionals. That doesn't mean that tournament players aren't capable of making great reads and great plays.

This is not unlike amateur golfers who may hit great shots, but not as often as the top professionals. Plus, the amateurs' bad shots can be extremely bad.

Why do many of the same players do well in tournaments year after year? The main reason is that they are the ones playing in the most tournaments. If a record of entries were kept and a "batting average" were computed, the results would be more reflective of skill levels. Using a baseball analogy, let's say that finishing in the money is a single, finishing at the final table is a

double, finishing in second place or third place is a triple, and winning is a home run. It is hard for a person with 20 at bats for the year to get as many total bases as someone who has 150 at bats.

Why aren't more complete records kept? It's in the best interest of the people who run tournaments, publish magazines, and produce television programs to promulgate the myth that the most successful tournament players are the best players. This provides a greater incentive for players to enter tournaments and enhances the tournament as a product. As the famous tournament director Jack McClelland once confided, "We are selling the idea that these are the greatest players in the world."

In major tournaments, the final no-limit hold'em event has the highest buy-in and the highest payout. It is the event that is most often televised. A lot of bad plays are made. One reason is that no-limit hold'em isn't played very often except in tournaments, so the players don't get much practice. Also, only selected hands are shown on television. Some plays may not be as bad as they look, since viewers don't have complete knowledge of what happened on preceding hands. Players will put their opponents on a hand and go with their feelings. It is easy to second guess the plays while looking at all the hole cards, the way they are shown on television.

Tournaments

TOURNAMENT STRATEGY

When I play in a no-limit hold'em tournament, I usually play solidly for the first few levels until the structure changes to one with antes in addition to blinds. I try to set up my opponents so that I am able to successfully run some risky bluffs. If I have built up a conservative image, I raise more liberally in late position and occasionally resteal when I think players in late position are trying to steal my blinds.

If the no-limit tournament has a rebuy period at the beginning, I use a different strategy. I play like a maniac during the rebuy period and hope my opponents don't adjust to my more rational play after the rebuy period is over. You should copy this strategy only if there is significant extrinsic value in winning the tournament, and you can afford to rebuy whenever it is allowed. Before embarking on these image-based strategies, I make sure I am not playing at a table that will be breaking up in the early rounds.

In no-limit tournaments, I separate my opponents into two categories: ones I can run over and ones who will call me down with marginal hands. I'm also acutely aware of who has more chips than I have and who has

less. There is a safety net when a hand can be played without the possibility of going broke, but it is dangerous when one mishap can cause elimination.

A common lament of unsuccessful tournament players is, "I get close, but I just can't seem to get over the hump." Generally, they play a style that guarantees they will be short on chips when they get close to a money-paying position. Most players play to survive instead of to build up their chips. They are afraid to call a raiser and take a flop because they feel it's too dangerous. They hope to pick up the blinds once a round so they can maintain their chip position. This strategy often enables them to finish in the top half of the field or barely make it into the money. (In a tournament, normally the top ten percent of the field make the money, while 60% to 70% of the prize pool is split among the top three finishers.) It is better to play a volatile style that yields two finishes in the top five percent of the field and eight finishes in the bottom fifty, for every ten tournaments played. When I play, I often feel as if I am in a race to get the chip lead at my table. I will try to steal any pot, before the flop or after, if I sense weakness in my opponents.

Tournaments

Regardless of style, players in tournaments find themselves short-chipped relative to the blinds much more often than in side games. Whenever I have less than ten times the big blind, I consider myself to be low on chips. In that situation, I move all-in before the flop on any hand I choose to play. My hand selection also changes. Playing small suited-connectors isn't profitable when I am unable to invest a small amount of money to beat big pairs out of a large amount after the flop. Hands like King-Jack offsuit are now playable for all of my chips in middle position, whereas I would have been afraid to play them with more chips in front of me because I couldn't *stand a raise*, that is, I would have

been unable to call a reraise before the flop. If I am in late position and no one has entered the pot, I raise all-in with any hand containing an Ace whenever I have less than ten times the big blind. I generalize this short-chip strategy to include situations where I am not low on chips, but I'm in late position and every player behind me has less than ten times the big blind. Instead of making the typical three-times-the-big-blind raise, I raise enough to cover my opponents. But when I have a pair of Aces, I make an exception to this rule. I make a smaller raise to entice someone behind me to try to bully me out of the pot with a reraise.

When I get knocked out of a tournament, I try not to dwell on the final hand. I realize that if I had accrued more chips by playing better, or at least differently, I would have had more chips than the person who busted me. If, somewhere along the way, I got all-in with the worst hand and survived, I feel as if I was freerolling from that point on. If I was all-in twice on hands where I was a 2 to 1 favorite, I was freerolling. If I survived three 4 to 1 favorites – hands where I had pair over pair before the flop, five outs against me on the flop, or one pair against undercards before the flop – then I was about even money to have been knocked out.

TOP TEN INGREDIENTS NEEDED TO WIN POKER TOURNAMENTS

10. **Perseverance.** Even when short chipped, don't give up. Instead, look for the best opportunity to steal or double up. Also, you must try not to get worn down when you go through a streak of barely out-of-the-money finishes. It is usually disappointing to end up in any position except the top three, since the payoffs for the other places pale in comparison.

9. **Ability to manipulate bad players.** Many weak players take a shot at tournaments. You must understand what hands their bets represent and what they will do. (Analogy: Someone who is considered a great communicator may not be able to communicate with children as well as a good elementary school teacher can.)

8. **Flexibility to change speeds.** The faster the limits increase, the more active you have to be in accruing chips. In tournaments, there are times you will not play a hand because you have a loose table image and can't stand a raise. At other times, you know you can steal or play back because your opponents think you are playing tight.

7. **Ability to focus.** It is necessary to focus and concentrate for long periods of time. When playing in a side game, you can take short breaks to give your brain a rest. Even when you are out of a hand in a tournament, you should watch the play of unfamiliar players who are at your table. You should make a quick study of them so you have an idea of their capabilities. In side games, there isn't the same urgency to learn the style and possible moves of a new player.

6. **Familiarity with opponents.** As you play in more tournaments, you will gain experience with the players who frequent the tournament circuit. It's a big advantage to know who to bluff and who not to, and who will not try to bluff you. When a player bets into you unexpectedly, is it a bluff, a value-bet, or a strong bet? If you had played with him a few times, you would probably know his pattern. Without that experience, you will have to guess.

5. **Skill at chip-dependent strategy.** When you have more chips than the other players at the table, you should use them like a bludgeon. Remember, everybody except one person is going to lose all his chips. Your opponents are not necessarily competing to win chips, but to go broke slower than almost everyone else. They often will not commit themselves and will try to avoid confrontations. When

players are trying to hang on so they can get to the next payoff amount, you can apply extra pressure.

4. **Skill with small bets.** This applies primarily to no-limit tournaments. Use smaller bets than you would in side games. They will usually have the same effect because in a tournament everyone is relatively short-stacked and can't rebuy. In limit poker as well as in no-limit, good players avoid over-committing chips to a pot because they don't want their fate determined by the result of one hand.

3. **Starting at good tables.** An initial table with weak players is a big factor in winning a tournament. This may enable you to get off to a good start so you can attack smaller stacks and survive after some losing hands.

2. **Having a good run of cards.** To win a tournament, you will have to win most of the time when you have the best of it, and some of the time when you have the worst of it. You will be involved in key hands that you must win each time the limits increase.

1. **Entering a lot of tournaments.** You can't win if you don't play.

HYPOTHETICAL BET

Philosophers who lived several hundred years ago are now known for their ridiculous discussions, such as, "How many angels can fit on the head of a pin?" Gamblers get into similar arguments and may even bet on them. Here is a typical hypothetical bet that you might hear: In the future, what if there was enough sponsorship money for tournaments so all the side-game players would compete? Suppose a ten-event tournament composed of the ten most prevalent forms of poker was held. How would the winning high-stakes players fare against the current best tournament players?

First, too many players would enter, which would make it impossible to have such an event without some qualifying system. Second, the added money would have to be at least ten million dollars so all the big-limit players would have an incentive to qualify.

I think we would see an even mix of higher-limit players and top tournament professionals. Some tournament players have styles well-suited to tournaments and are better at the skills mentioned in the top ten list. You might think that a professional side-game player could easily change his style, but it is easier said than done. It's like trying to change one's golf swing.

If the event were held again a year later, the winning side-game players would probably do better, since they would have had more time to practice their tournament strategy.

If, on the other hand, the top tournament players were able to get sponsored to play in the big-limit side games, they would not do very well. There would be a feeding frenzy until the money ran out.

Ace on the River

Note

I wrote the first draft of the previous chapter in 2003 at a time when I had only traveled to nearby tournament sites to play in side games. At that time, I had played in about fifty events in my life and had come in first three times. The *World Poker Tour* ushered in a new era in poker which induced many side-game players to play in more tournament events. Since then, I have traveled across the country and to Europe for the sole purpose of playing in poker tournaments. I played in around 100 events in 2003 and 2004, and I am often recognized as a top tournament player, even though I still make my living playing in side games.

CHAPTER 27

SOME
NO-LIMIT
TOURNAMENT
HANDS

"Those who lack courage will always find a philosophy to justify it."

Albert Camus
(1913-1960),
French writer and philosopher

"The most important thing in science is not so much to obtain new facts as to discover new ways of thinking about them."

Sir William Bragg
(1862-1942),
Australian physicist — 1915
Nobel Prize laureate in physics

Ace on the River

THIS CHAPTER CONTAINS SOME HANDS FROM
TOURNAMENTS IN WHICH I HAVE PLAYED.
I SUGGEST YOU READ IT SLOWLY,
TAKING TIME TO ANSWER THE QUESTIONS ON
EACH ODD-NUMBERED PAGE.
AFTER YOU HAVE DECIDED HOW YOU
WOULD ANSWER EACH QUESTION,
TURN THE PAGE AND READ MY ANALYSIS.

Some No-Limit Tournament Hands

TOURNAMENT HAND 1: BORGATA $10,000 *World Poker Tour* EVENT. SEPTEMBER 19, 2004

An older gentleman, Alex Milan, had been playing a lot of hands and playing them passively. He checked and called some sizable bets with top pair with a weak kicker, and also with second pair, with varied results. All players started this event with 20,000 in chips. When the following hand came up, Alex had 18,000 in chips and I had around 21,000.

The blinds were 100 and 200. Alex opened in first position for 500. A player two to his left called. I was on the button and looked down to the pleasant sight of

Play the hand for me. Would you raise, and if so, how much?

(Determine an amount before turning the page.)

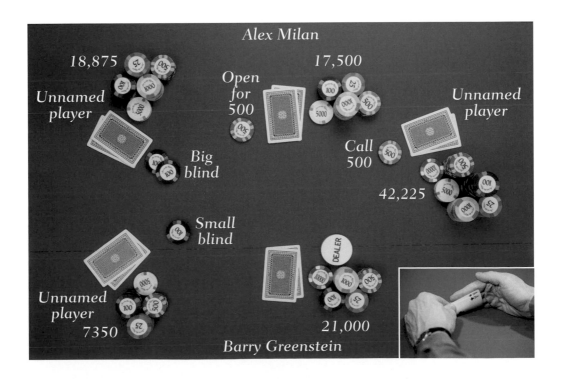

Ace on the River

It is wrong to slow-play against a "calling station," i.e., a player who doesn't bluff a lot but frequently calls. Also, you don't want to make it easy for the players in the blinds to call. You want to make Alex and the caller pay a price to draw against your hand.

Before you decide how much to raise, you should count the pot. Including the 500 you will put into the pot before you raise, the size of the pot is 1800.

A pre-flop raise of slightly more than the pot is normal. If you raise less than that, you will be letting Alex and the other player in too cheaply. You also want to raise an amount that leaves room for your opponents to reraise. In this case, you don't expect a reraise because Alex is a passive player.

All in all, you should put about 2500 in the pot, which is a raise of 2000. If you raise more than 3000, both players are likely to fold. If you raise less than 1500, they will probably call, but the small raise will make them tread lightly, afraid that you are enticing them into the pot because you have Aces.

Assume you raised 2000, Alex called, and the other player folded.

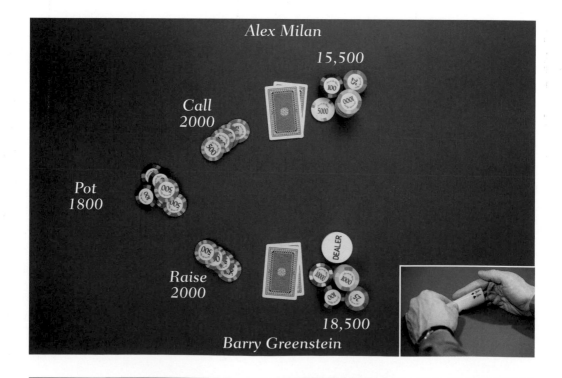

Some No-Limit Tournament Hands

The flop comes:

Alex checks to you.

How much should you bet?

If you are called, what figures to be the best turn card for you?

What are some bad turn cards for you?

Is there any point in speculating about the turn cards before they come?

Ace on the River

In a side game, a pot-sized bet would be typical. In tournaments, conserving chips is more critical when there is no option to rebuy, and chip stacks are usually low relative to the size of the blinds. Therefore, a bet of around two-thirds the size of the pot is normal. At this point, the pot is 5800, so 4000 is a good amount to bet.

Alex calls the 4000 with only a slight hesitation. If he flopped a set or top two pair, you will probably double him up. If he flopped a straight draw, you are making him pay the price to draw. Most likely, he made a pair of Kings.

The best turn card for you is a Deuce. This limits his outs to two if he paired the King. If he flopped top two pair, you will have outdrawn him.

An Ace on the turn may prevent him from losing any more money if he called on the flop after pairing his King. Also, he will make a straight if he has Queen-Jack.

A Nine may make him a straight or give him some extra outs if he has King-Queen or King-Jack.

A Ten on the turn would give him three Tens if he called on the flop with second pair.

A King is certainly the worst card for you since his most frequent calling hand on the flop is top pair.

Some No-Limit Tournament Hands

It is helpful to speculate about cards before they come so you are prepared with your action on the next street. Most players don't think about what cards may come up. Even after the cards are dealt, some players wait until it is their turn before they start thinking about what to do. That makes them very readable. I am usually prepared with my play before it is my turn to act, and I try to decide how I will respond to any action my opponent may take.

The turn brings:

This is the single best card in the deck for you, since it doesn't open up any flush draws.

Alex checks to you. He has 11,500 left in front of him.

How much should you bet?

Ace on the River

The pot is now 13,800. The Deuce is such a nice card that your main concern should be extracting the maximum amount from your opponent. If you bet the amount he has in front of him, you may scare him into folding. Even if you bet 9000 or 10,000, he will become aware that his tournament life is in the balance and may fold so he can continue to play.

The correct bet here is 5000 or 6000.

If he calls, you can bet the rest on the river. He will probably feel that there is too much money in the pot to fold. If a King comes on the river, you played well but were very unlucky.

The betting on this hand illustrates an important difference in my thought process when playing limit poker versus no-limit. In limit poker, I try to decide what my hand is worth: "Should I check and fold if my opponent bets?" "Is the hand worth a call, a bet, or a raise?" When I play no-limit poker, I am often more concerned with what I think my opponent's hand is worth. If I have a good hand and want him to call my bet, I try to figure out the maximum I can bet and get called. If I have a weak hand and don't want to get called, I try to figure out the minimum I can bet that will cause him to fold. I paraphrase this concept by saying, "In limit poker I play my hand. In no-limit I play my opponent's hand."

Some No-Limit Tournament Hands

What actually happened at the table?

Alex called my raise of 2000 before the flop and my bet of 4000 on the flop. I was convinced he had a King and was unlikely to fold on the turn. I decided to bet 6000, but when I reached for my chips I saw I had a 10,000 chip and three 1000 chips. I contemplated whether to put the 10,000 chip in the pot and announce the bet as 6000. Then, deciding he would probably call the 10,000 anyway, I put the chip into the pot without stating an amount. After separating 10,000 from his stack and staring at the measly 1500 that he would have left if he called, Alex studied for about three minutes. Finally, he showed K♦ Q♦ and threw his cards face down toward the dealer. I probably cost myself 11,500 by not being careful.

Some No-Limit Tournament Hands

TOURNAMENT HAND 2: *World Series of Poker* **FINAL EVENT (SECOND DAY) MAY 14, 1996**

The structure is 400 and 800 blinds with 100 ante. Lucy Rokach, with around 60,000 in chips, opens for 2500 in early position. I consider Lucy to be the best female no-limit hold'em player in the world. I would classify her play as somewhat aggressive, but not overly aggressive. Everyone folds to me.

I am in the big blind with

I have 32,000 in chips in addition to the blind and the ante I have already put into the pot.

What would you do in my position?

Would it make any difference if I only had 8000 in chips?

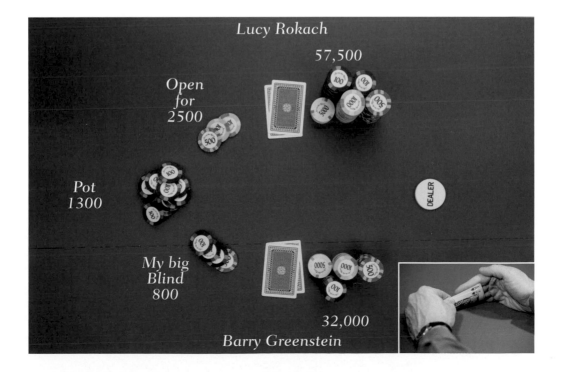

Ace on the River

It is right to call and take a flop. This is a nice drawing hand. It's too dangerous to raise a player who has opened in early position. If I raise 10,000, Lucy may reraise me all-in and I will have to fold.

If I only had 8000, it would be better to take a shot here by moving all-in. It will cost me too big a percentage of my chips to call and then fold when the flop is bad.

Assume I call.

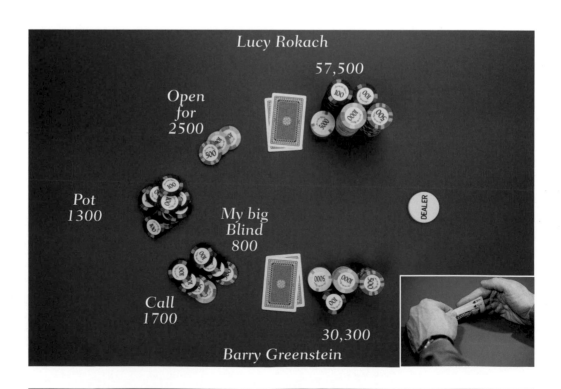

Some No-Limit Tournament Hands

The flop is

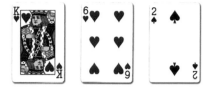

I am first to act. What should I do?

Should I play differently if I only had 10,000 left in front of me?

In the situation where I have around 30,000 left, I think it is best to check since the pre-flop raiser in a heads-up pot will normally bet on the flop with any hand. Then, regardless of the size of Lucy's bet, I will check-raise all-in. Lucy will probably fold if she has King-Jack or worse. If I move in without waiting for Lucy to bet, I would be missing out on the 4000 or 5000 she is likely to bet on the flop. If she calls, I will probably have to draw out. I am a slight underdog against King-Queen and a favorite against a pair lower than Jacks. I am less than a 2 to 1 underdog against Aces, and less than a 3 to 1 underdog against a set.

If I only had 10,000 left in front of me, it would be better to go all-in without waiting for Lucy to bet. I would rather win the pot right there than risk having her call with an underpair because she is pot-committed.

Some No-Limit Tournament Hands

What actually happened at the table?

I raised 8000 before the flop and Lucy reraised all-in. I folded.

Since I wanted to have a flop in this example, I combined the hand I played against Lucy with one I misplayed against David Rubin during the 1992 *World Series of Poker* to produce Tournament Hand 2. In the hand with David, the flop came as indicated above. David had 15,000 left, and the pot was a little over 10,000. I checked my flush draw on the flop and David bet 8000. I raised him all-in and, after thinking for over a minute, he called with a pair of Jacks. If I had moved in on the flop, he probably would have folded. I didn't hit an Ace or a heart and lost 20,000 on the hand.

Some No-Limit Tournament Hands

TOURNAMENT HAND 3: SUPERSTARS INVITATIONAL AT THE PALMS, ROUND 2 JUNE 3, 2004

The blinds are 3000 and 6000, and the ante is 500. There are four players left. Gus Hansen, a talented loose player, brings it in from the button for 19,000. He has 395,000 in chips. I am in the big blind with 215,000 in chips.

My hand is

What should I do?

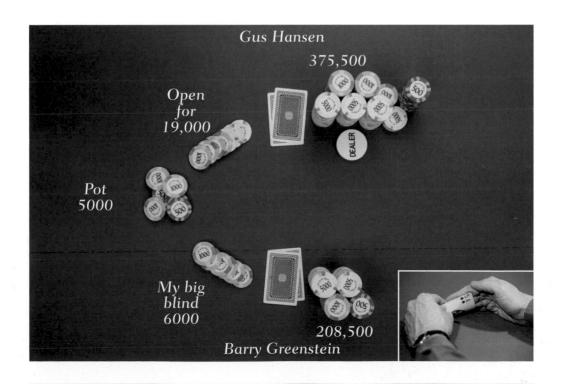

Even though a raise will often allow me to pick up the pot before the flop against a loose player, it is better to raise with strong hands hoping to get called, or with very weak hands in an effort to resteal. I don't want to deprive myself of an opportunity to double-up against a player who frequently plays weak suited hands when I have a suited Ace. I recommend calling here.

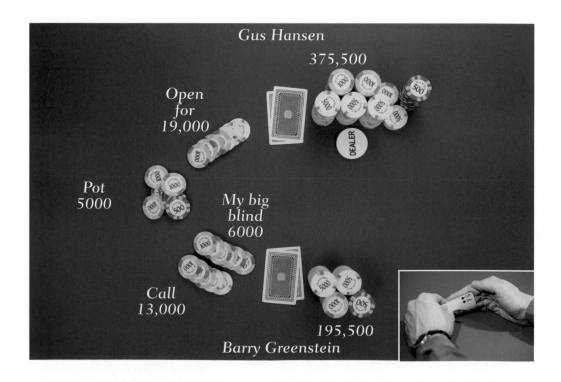

Some No-Limit Tournament Hands

The flop comes:

What should I do now?

The pot size is 43,000. If I had less than 60,000, I might bet all-in instead of checking. Since I have around 200,000 in chips, I will check to the expected bet by Gus and then make a sizable raise in an attempt to win the pot on the flop. If I get called, I will probably be a slight underdog against a pair or a huge favorite against a flush draw or a straight draw.

Some No-Limit Tournament Hands

I check and Gus makes a surprising check behind me.
What kind of hand could he possibly have?

The flop looks dangerous, although he may have no piece of it. But Gus is a good player who will usually bet on the flop when he has the betting lead. Maybe he is setting a trap. If he paired one of the cards on the flop, he probably would have bet, because he wouldn't want to give a free card that might be an overcard.

Even if he had flopped two pair or a set, it would be normal for him to bet with so many possible draws on a board like this. He would not want to give me a free card in case I hold Queen-Jack or Jack-Nine. With these hands, I might put a lot of my chips in on the flop, but I may avoid losing any chips if he checks on the flop and I miss on the turn.

When a good player raises in and then checks on the flop, it is suspicious. I always proceed carefully, allowing for the possibility that he has an unbeatable hand on the flop — in this case, a straight.

The turn is

What should I do now?

I could make a small bet, and if Gus has nothing he will fold. But if I check, he may bluff since I have checked to him twice. The board has become even more dangerous with this pairing flush card. If I bet, it is unlikely that Gus will raise here unless he has a full house. I recommend checking again.

Some No-Limit Tournament Hands

Gus bets 15,000.

Should I call or raise?

Gus Hansen

360,500

Bet
15,000

Pot
43,000

DEALER

195,500

Barry Greenstein

If I had position on him, it might be better to call. But I have to act first, and I am afraid he will check behind me if I call here and check on the river. Also, I want to build the pot for a big payoff on the river.

It is likely that Gus would have made a token bet on the flop even if he had flopped a set, so my flush is probably good. The pot is 73,000 including his bet and my call. A raise of 30,000 to 50,000 will get more money in the pot and validate that he checked on the flop as a trap.

I raise 31,000. Gus calls. If he flopped a straight, he will be ripe to call a big bet on the river. He may find it difficult to imagine that I have a flush, since he may decide I might have bet the flop or the turn with the hand I have. He may think that he confused me with his check on the flop, but in reality he will fall into his own trap.

Some No-Limit Tournament Hands

The river is

What now?

Ace on the River

The river was certainly a disgusting card. Even if the flush is good, it will be hard to get called for much now. Most players would check. Still, Gus may think that my raise on the turn was a bluff, so I might as well make a bet on the river. There are a few hands I can beat with which he may call a bet: an overpair, a straight, a small flush, possibly even an Ace with a big spade. I want to make a bet big enough to look like a bluff, but small enough to get called. I am hoping he thinks I am continuing a bluff that I made on the turn, or that I missed with a semi-bluff while holding the lone Ace of spades.

The pot is 135,000, but a bet of between 40,000 and 70,000 may be all I can hope to get Gus to call.

Some No-Limit Tournament Hands

What actually happened at the table?

I played this hand at the table exactly the way I recommended. I bet 50,000 on the river. Gus called after thinking for almost a minute. He had 9♥ 7♥ and had flopped a straight.

If he had bet the flop, I would have gotten my money in, and he would have been as almost a 2 to 1 favorite. As it was, if a fourth spade didn't come or the board hadn't paired again on the river, he would have lost most of his chips. I would then have been a big favorite to win the second round of this tournament.

After this hand, I lost a few small pots and then got all-in with Queen-Jack against Gus's Queen-Eight on a flop of K-Q-4. Gus hit an Eight on the river to knock me out.

Some No-Limit Tournament Hands

Tournament Hand 4: *World Series of Poker* $2000 Pot-limit Hold'em. May 10, 2004

We were only 45 minutes into the first level, 25 and 50 blinds, when I picked up

in early position. I opened for 150, and each player folded up to the small blind, a player named Nathan Brandon. Nathan, with whom I had never played before, confidently raised 350, which was the size of the pot. He started the hand with 2200 in chips and had been in only two previous pots. This was the first raise he had made. I hadn't played many hands either, but I had won a pot and had 2600 in chips at the start of this hand.

What should I do?

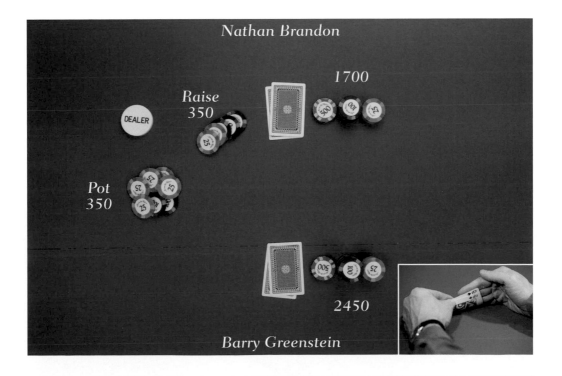

Ace on the River

Most players won't play for all their chips before the flop early in a tournament unless they have two Aces or two Kings. I am willing to get my chips in with lesser hands if I think the situation is right, but based on my observations, Nathan appeared to be a conservative player. Under the circumstances, this hand is worth calling, taking a flop, and folding to a bet after the flop if an overcard comes. If small cards come on the flop, it will be hard to avoid losing more money on this hand if I am beat.

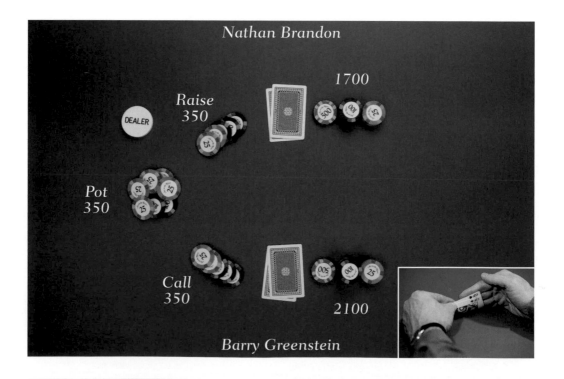

Some No-Limit Tournament Hands

After calling 350, the flop comes with the beautiful Queen of hearts as the first card off of the deck. The Ace of spades comes behind it. This is a great card for me if Nathan has Ace-King, but a disastrous card if he started with pocket Aces.

The complete flop:

Much to my surprise, Nathan checks.

What is going on here?

How much should I bet?

Ace on the River

If Nathan had Ace-King, it would be normal for him to make a decent-sized bet. He might check with a pair of Jacks or Tens because of the two overcards. He might check with a pair of Kings because of the Ace on the flop. And, of course, he might check trying to fool me if he flopped a set of Aces.

If he had made a sizable bet, it would be right just to call and hope I can get him to put the rest of his money in on the turn. But since he checked, the only logical hand he could have which would make it correct for me to bet is two Kings. If this were the case, a bet here would prevent Nathan from getting a free card. However, even if he has two Kings and I decide to check, I may be able to milk him for a few chips on the turn or the river if I can convince him I don't like the Ace on the board either. I think the correct action here is a check.

Some No-Limit Tournament Hands

Let's assume I check. The turn card is the 2♦.

The board shows:

Flop   Turn

Nathan makes a strange bet of only 250 into a pot of 1050.

What should I do now?

Ace on the River

I don't see how his bet has altered the concerns I had on the flop. It seems best to call the small bet.

Nathan Brandon

1450

Bet 250

DEALER

Pot 1050

Call 250

1850

Barry Greenstein

The river is the 5♠.

The board reads:

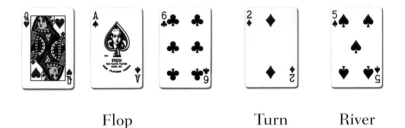

| Flop | Turn | River |

Now Nathan lunges forward as he pushes his remaining 1450 into the pot.

What are his possible hands?

Ace on the River

It's hard to imagine any hand other than pocket Aces that would be bet in this fashion. It certainly seems right to fold.

What actually happened at the table?

The play went as indicated. I studied for two minutes, trying to come up with a reason to call. Finally, logic prevailed, and I threw my hand toward the muck. Nathan, in a nice gesture, flashed his pocket Aces. I grabbed my cards from the edge of the muck and "triumphantly" displayed my pocket Queens, which sent the table into a minor frenzy.

Some No-Limit Tournament Hands

TOURNAMENT HAND 5: *World Series of Poker* Final Event (Second Day) May 24, 2004

The blinds are 250 and 500, and the ante is 50. I have 40,000 in chips, and I am one to the right of the button. All three players to my left have less than 25,000.

Everyone ahead of me folds, and I pick up

I have been the most aggressive player at the table thus far.

What should I do?

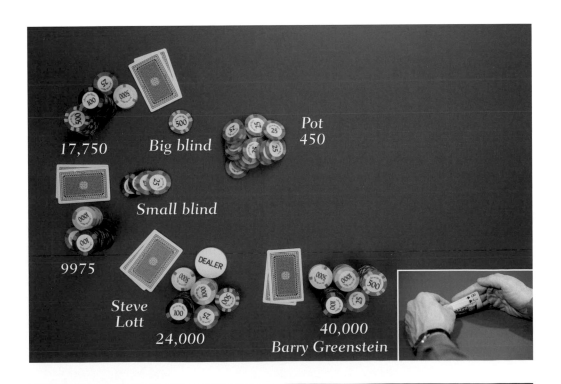

17,750

Big blind

Pot
450

Small blind

9975

DEALER

Steve
Lott

24,000

40,000
Barry Greenstein

Ace on the River

If there were no antes, there would not be enough in the pot to warrant playing this hand. If any of the players had more chips than I have, I would attempt a steal only if I felt confident that none of the three opponents to my left were capable of reraising me on a bluff. If one of them had more chips than I have, it would not only make it easier for him to raise me with a marginal hand before the flop, but it may also restrict the types of plays I will be able to make after the flop.

In this example, even though my opponents may suspect that I am stealing, I like to keep the pressure on them when I am in late position. They will usually fold marginal hands when one wrong move will cause them to be knocked out of a big tournament. A normal raise is three times the big blind, or a little more than that when there are antes as well as blinds. With this structure, I suggest making an opening bet of around 1600.

On the button is Steve Lott, an excellent professional player from Texas. He calls and both blinds fold. He started the hand with around 24,000 in chips.

Pot
1200

Call
1600

Open
for
1600

Steve
Lott

22,400

38,400
Barry Greenstein

Some No-Limit Tournament Hands

The flop is:

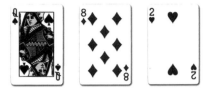

I am first to act.

What should I do now?

At this point, the pot is 4400. Even if I hadn't flopped a pair, a bet of around 3000 would be reasonable.

I bet 3000 and hope that Steve folds. He calls quickly. The turn card is the 9♠.

The board now shows:

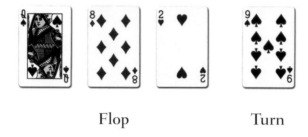

Flop   Turn

Some No-Limit Tournament Hands

I am sure I am beat. Steve knows that I'm an aggressive player and may call any bet if he has a Queen, hoping to catch me bluffing. I check and Steve bets 4500.

What should I do?

Ace on the River

Some hands Steve may have are King-Queen, Queen-Jack suited, or a pair of Tens. He could have a set of Eights, but that is unlikely. Also, he might have turned a set of Nines. With Ace-Queen, or a pair of Queens or better, he probably would have raised before the flop. If he had called with Jack-Ten suited before the flop, he may have decided against calling 3000 on the flop with a gut-shot draw. And even if he did call to hit a gut-shot, it normally would have taken him a few seconds to make that decision.

If this were a side game, it would be correct to fold to Steve's bet. In a tournament, however, I think it is correct to move him all-in. Very few players are capable of making a gutsy play such as this. It will appear to Steve that I have a straight, a set, an overpair, or at least Ace-Queen. These hands should be bet the same way as the semi-bluff in the actual hand. Aggressive plays like this enable one to amass chips in a tournament. Passive players inevitably find themselves too short-chipped to operate. Notice that Steve can't have top pair and a flush draw since the Queen on the board is the suit of the possible flush draw.

If I get called, I still have some outs. I will win with a Ten and probably with a Jack or an Eight as well.

What actually happened at the table?

The play went as I described, but on the turn I chickened out and folded to Steve's 4500 bet. Over the course of the next few rounds, I lost some small pots and within thirty minutes my chip stack had dwindled to around 8000. I went all-in with Ace-Nine on the button, and the player in the small blind busted me with his two Queens.

Some No-Limit Tournament Hands

Tournament Hand 6: Plaza Ultimate Poker Challenge Final Event. October 29, 2004

The blinds are 50 and 100. We started with 5000 in chips and are at the third level. Eighty players remain out of the hundred who started. I have 7150 in chips, which is slightly above average. Our table is seven-handed. The player to my right folds, and I am next to act with Q♠ J♠. I open for 300. I am called by "Miami" John Cernuto, an accomplished tournament player who has 3000 in chips, and also by Jeff Stoff, who is on the button with around 16,000 in chips. Jeff has been playing very carefully. A couple of rounds earlier he had Ace-King and didn't raise my opening bet. He is one of the chip leaders as a result of winning a few pots with big pocket pairs that stood up. Melissa Pearl, a relatively inexperienced player in the big blind who has been playing somewhat conservatively, goes all-in for 1250 more.

What are the considerations for each of the four possible plays?

Which one should I choose?

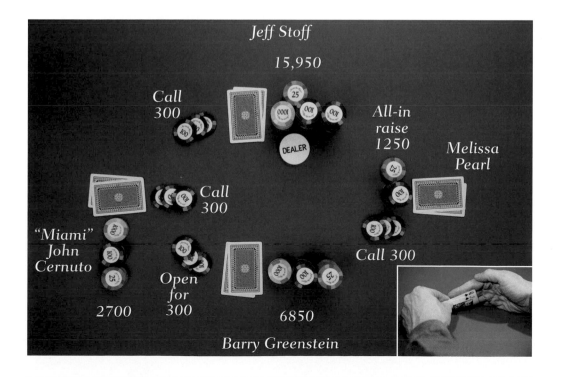

Ace on the River

Play 1. *Fold.*

The Q♠ J♠ may be a sizable underdog against the all-in raiser unless she has a pair of Tens or lower. It might be better to get out with a small loss on the hand, since calling or raising may lead to bigger losses.

Play 2. *Call.*

I will be getting 2 to 1 pot odds on my call, or 3 to 1 odds if another player calls. Unfortunately, I might be an underdog against any hand that calls behind me, and I leave myself open to the possibility of getting raised out of the pot by Jeff.

Play 3. *Raise all-in.*

This should shut out John and Jeff unless they have Ace-King or a pair of Jacks or better. These hands are almost impossible for John to have and are unlikely for Jeff to have. John would certainly have raised with any of these hands since he is somewhat short on chips. (There is a small possibility that John has Aces and has slowplayed his hand to try to get additional action behind him.) The issue is: if I get John and Jeff to fold, will I be less than a 2 to 1 underdog against likely hands that Melissa has?

Here are the approximate odds against Q♠ J♠ winning versus some possible hands that Melissa may have:

A♠ A♥	4.4 to 1	A♦ A♣	4.1 to 1
K♠ K♥	4.8 to 1	K♦ K♣	4.5 to 1
Q♥ Q♣	5.3 to 1		
J♥ J♣	1.7 to 1		

Pair of Tens or lower is approximately even.

A♥ K♥	1.7 to 1	A♠ K♥	1.6 to 1
A♥ K♣	1.5 to 1	A♥ Q♥	2.3 to 1
A♠ Q♥	2.3 to 1	A♥ Q♣	2.2 to 1
A♥ J♥	2.3 to 1	A♠ J♥	2.3 to 1
A♥ J♣	2.2 to 1	A♥ 10♥	1.4 to 1
A♠ 10♥	1.3 to 1	A♥ 10♣	1.2 to 1

Some No-Limit Tournament Hands

If Melissa is unlikely to move in with Ace-Ten or small pairs, these numbers point slightly towards folding. But in a tournament, a player can add volatility by playing in pots where he still has plenty of chips if he loses, as long as he is getting close to the correct pot odds.

Play 4. *Raise an intermediate amount.*

A raise of 2000 may scare Jeff out if he has Jacks or Tens, since this is the kind of raise I would tend to make with Aces or Kings. If I raise all-in, he may be more likely to call since it looks like a shut-out play with something like Ace-King or Ace-Queen.

Although folding may be the best choice, let's assume I raise 2000. John folds, but Jeff gives me the unpleasant surprise of an all-in raise.

What should I do now?

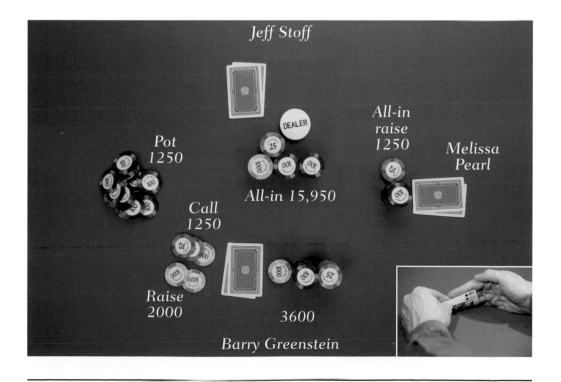

Ace on the River

There is 5000 in the main pot and 4000 in the side pot before Jeff's raise. I have 3600 remaining. If I call and win the side pot, I will have 11,200 in chips. If I also win the main pot, I will have 16,200 in chips. Conventional wisdom says I should fold and "live to fight another day." The theory is that as long as you are still in, even with a short stack, you have a chance. Besides, you don't have to get all the chips to make a nice profit in a tournament. You just need to hang in long enough to get a share of the prize pool.

I would be more inclined to fold if that choice would leave me with average or better in chips. Average chips at this point was more than 6000. Another important consideration is the strength of the other players at the table. If I am at a "good" table, it would be more reasonable to fold, since I will have a positive expectation with the remaining 3600. If I am at a "tough" table, it makes more sense to take a shot here to get a lot of chips.

Although the power of the short stack is a well-accepted principle (see the *Money Management* chapter), I have found in practice that once I get a chip lead on the players at my table, I am easily able to exploit the weakness in their "survival" strategy. It may even be worth it to take slightly the worst of it to get a chip lead, especially given the fact that payouts are very top-heavy in tournaments.

What actually happened at the table?

I was shocked when Jeff reraised me and, influenced by his earlier non-raise with Ace-King, I decided to fold. I now think it was the wrong decision since all the players at my table seemed to be competent.

I didn't know the odds of all the hands against Q♠ J♠, but I knew I was around a 2 to 1 underdog against a strong Ace or around even money against smaller pairs. I could also be a favorite if Melissa was somehow just taking a shot to get good odds on her money. That wasn't my read in this case, but I have seen players make this play on hands such as Jack-Ten suited.

I was glad I folded when Jeff turned over two Queens, the worst match-up for me. To make matters worse for my hand, Melissa showed A♠ A♦. My satisfaction was quickly erased when three spades flopped and no spade came on the turn or the river. As I reassessed my decisions, I was left to wonder if I was just "playing results."

I didn't pick up any good hands the next few rounds and was out of the tournament within the hour.

Some No-Limit Tournament Hands

TOURNAMENT HAND 7: THIS IS A SCENARIO THAT COMES UP FREQUENTLY IN TOURNAMENTS.

The blinds are 100 and 200, and the ante is 25. Eight players are at the table. Two players fold and the next player, with more than 10,000 in chips, opens for 600. You have 4500 — not a lot of chips, but enough so you are not in desperation mode yet. You pick up one of these hands:

What are the possible plays for hands of this strength and which play would you choose?

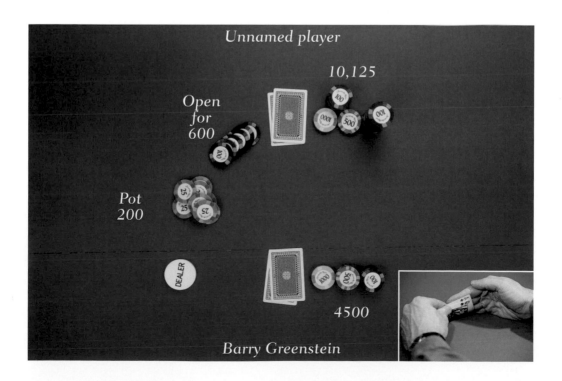

Ace on the River

Play 1. *Fold.*

This might be the correct play against a tight player, but you probably can't afford to wait for a better situation.

Play 2. *Call and hope to get a helpful flop.*

This is the play that most players make. They are not sure if they should fold or raise, so they call instead. I don't like to do this against a player who is likely to bet regardless of what comes on the flop, since it will cause me to be frequently outplayed when I have the best hand. If I continue on, only when I get a helpful flop, I will fold most of the time and bleed off more than 10% of my chips.

Play 3. *Raise approximately the size of the pot.*

At this juncture, the pot size is 500 in blinds and antes, 600 for the opening bet, and if I'm going to play, we include my call of 600 in the calculation of the size of the pot. Therefore, the pot size is 1700 before I raise. If I raise 2000 and my opponent reraises me all-in for my last 1900, there will be 1700 + 2000 + 2000 + 1900 = 7600 in the pot when I have to decide whether to call. I will be getting 4 to 1 odds on a call of my last 1900. It is usually correct to call all-in before the flop when getting 4 to 1 odds except when neither card in the caller's hand is higher than the pair in the bettor's hand. For example, two Jacks is approximately a 4.4 to 1 favorite over two Nines. Two Kings is only a 2.1 to 1 favorite over Ace-Queen suited, but is more than a 4.5 to 1 favorite over Queen-Jack suited. (K♠ K♥ is an 18.8 to 1 favorite over K♦ 2♠, which is the largest disparity.)

Since the calculation above implies that it will normally be right to call an opponent's reraise, Play 3 does not seem like a good choice. The opener will reraise with a good hand, but when he has a marginal hand, an all-in raise by me will increase the chance of picking up the pot uncontested.

Some No-Limit Tournament Hands

Play 4. *Move all-in.*

This is the play I will usually make. (I normally make this play if I have less than eight times the opening raiser's bet.) If my opponent folds, I am happy to win the pot without a flop. Raising much larger than the size of the pot may convince my opponent to fold in some cases where he is a favorite or a slight underdog. I would also move in if I had Ace-King or pairs larger than Nines. I want to show my opponents that I will raise all-in with very strong hands so they will fold on occasions when my hand is not so strong. Sometimes, I will make this move on a bluff when my opponent raises from a position one to the right of the button or later, and I think he is stealing. But this type of resteal with such a short stack is normally too risky.

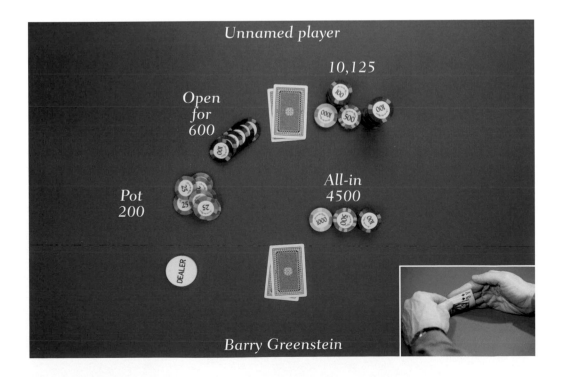

Unnamed player

10,125

Open for 600

All-in 4500

Pot 200

DEALER

Barry Greenstein

Some No-Limit Tournament Hands

TOURNAMENT HAND 8: *Jack Binion World Poker Open WPT Event. Final Day. January 29, 2004*

We were down to four handed. The blinds were 10,000 and 20,000, and the ante was 2000. Chip Reese was first to act. He moved all-in for 281,000. Randy Jensen, with 1.1 million in chips, folded on the button, James Tippin, also with around 1.1 million, called Chip's bet after a slight hesitation. I held

I had around 1.2 million in chips.

In this event, the payouts were

1st:	$1,278,370
2nd:	$656,460
3rd:	$328,230
4th:	$207,304

What should I do?

Ace on the River

I am not trying to be devious, but the right answer is: there is insufficient information to make a decision. This is one of the shortcomings of discussing hands without the benefit of "being at the table."

We need information about James Tippin.

1. Who is James Tippin and how does he play?

James Tippin is a retired carwash owner. I played with him for several hours the previous day. He made some loose calls with marginal hands. On Day Three of this four day event, he called a large pre-flop raise with A♣ 10♥. An Ace flopped. He check-called on the turn and the river and lost a fair amount of chips to a player holding A♠ K♥.

On another hand from the previous day, James had just won a nice pot from chip leader Randy Jensen. While James was still stacking his chips, he looked at his hand and brought it in for a normal raise. Randy appeared to be steaming and reraised. After a minute of thought, James reluctantly said, "All-in." Randy folded and James showed pocket Kings. I was surprised that his hand was this strong. It seemed like an easy reraise against Randy, who was clearly the loosest player at the table. Apparently James was willing to call some of his chips, but it took a hand this strong for him to put all his chips into the pot. James reraised only one other time, and that time he showed pocket Aces.

2. What did it appear he had when he called?

I surreptitiously studied James as he contemplated his call. If he had raised, I would have folded. Since he didn't raise, I assumed he had an Ace with a big kicker or a medium pair.

3. Are there any previous hands that could help me make the right decision?

Earlier, Chip Reese called for 12,000. Can Kim Hua, who eventually went out in fifth place, raised to 65,000 and James Tippin called. I had about 600,000 in chips and I held A♥ K♥. Can Kim Hua had about 200,000 more in chips, so I decided to raise to 300,000, which would set him in. Chip Reese and Can Kim Hua folded and James Tippin deliberated. While he was thinking, I realized that if I had moved all-in, it would probably have made it harder for him to call. As I studied him, I thought he had a hand like Ace-Queen suited or a pair of Tens. In this earlier hand, James finally called and the flop was

Some No-Limit Tournament Hands

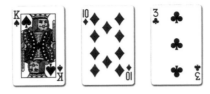

I decided I had to bet my last 300,000, expecting that if James called quickly he would show me a set of Tens. Fortunately, he "went in the tank" so I knew my hand was good. Then, he correctly folded. When the show aired, it was revealed that he held J♠ J♣. (Chip had called with A♣ 8♣ and Can Kim Hua had raised with 8♠ 8♥.)

Now let's get back to the hand in question. As I stated earlier, James called Chip's all-in bet and now it was up to me. When a player calls a sizable all-in bet and doesn't raise, it is very possible that he didn't raise because he has Aces and is hoping to lure an opponent behind him into the pot. James called, but he didn't appear confident that he was making the right choice. I didn't think he held Aces or Kings and was trying to trap me.

Armed with this additional information, what are the possible plays and which one would you choose?

Ace on the River

Play 1. *Fold.*

James is likely to have a better hand than Chip's. Chip would have raised all-in with an Ace and a small card. He would probably have gone all-in with a pair of Sixes or even Jack-Ten offsuit. If I fold, I will remain in good shape no matter who wins the pot. Ace-King suited is a nice hand, especially short-handed. I would fold only if I had a convincing tell that James was trapping with Aces or Kings.

Play 2. *Call.*

There are many tournament players who would call here, even if they suspected that they could raise James out of the pot. They want to allow for the maximum possibility of eliminating the short stack. Often, two players will call the short stack's all-in bet and then check on the flop, turn, and river, even with good hands. That prevents the short stack from benefiting when the best hand is bet out of the pot.

Let's say I raise and James folds. If Chip beats me, but James would have beaten Chip, Chip will have over 850,000 and will be back in contention instead of being eliminated.

If I call and don't hit an Ace or King, James may bet into me on the flop or on the turn and I may lose the chance to win the pot. Also, it would be painful to check it out, only to allow James to make a pair on the river and beat me.

Play 3. *Raise an intermediate amount.*

I could raise 400,000 or 500,000 to act as if I have Aces and I am hoping for a call. James may fall for this double-think and fold, while he might have called if I had bet all his chips.

Play 4. *Raise all-in.*

This should put the maximum pressure on James. If he doesn't have Aces or Kings, he has to be afraid that I have them. He will probably fold and hope that I can eliminate Chip. Although calling will increase the chances of knocking Chip out, raising and forcing James to fold will allow me to get 2 to 1 odds on my money, which will increase my chances of winning the tournament.

I raised all-in and James went into a prolonged study. At first, I thought he had a pair around Nines or Tens, and I was hoping he would fold. Then I remembered the call he had made the day before with Ace-Ten offsuit, and I thought he might be contemplating calling with Ace-Queen. If that was the case, I wanted a call.

I was wrong about the strength of James's hand. He had Q♦Q♣. I thought he was initially trying to decide whether to call or fold, but apparently he was trying to decide whether to call or raise.

Wouldn't it have been better for him to raise at his first opportunity and avoid getting into this predicament?

What should he do now?

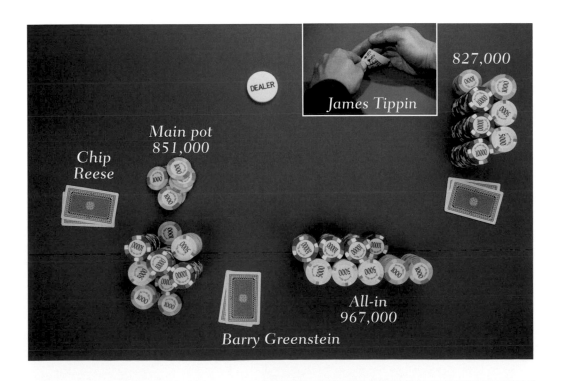

I would have raised all-in initially with James's hand to avoid having to guess what to do if I get a call behind me and then an Ace or King comes on the flop. Also, I would not want to entice the player behind me to move all-in, since I may have to fold and hope that he knocks the initial raiser out.

Even though I would have raised with James's hand, it doesn't necessarily mean that raising is the correct play for James to make with an aggressive player like me behind him. I can honestly say that I would have raised behind James with Ace-Queen suited or a pair of Jacks. If James had duped me into raising all-in with a pair of Tens or Jacks or with Ace-Queen, he would have been praised for outplaying me. I think it is right for James to call my raise here, even though it may result in him coming in fourth place if Chip wins the main pot and I win the side pot. Calling gives him a great shot at winning the tournament.

James called after five minutes of deliberation.

The diagram below shows the hands with the corresponding percentages.

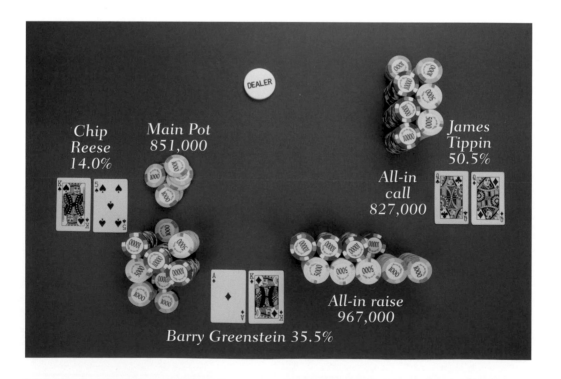

Some No-Limit Tournament Hands

James got his money in as a favorite against two of the biggest winners in poker history. If either James or I won this pot, we would be the odds-on favorite to win the tournament.

What happened at the table?

The play went as indicated. The flop, turn, and river were

James and Chip were knocked out, which gave me a 2,600,000 to 1,100,000 lead over Randy Jensen. I held better cards than Randy in our heads-up duel, and I went on to win the event.

James Tippin's play was criticized in several forums and articles. If he had won this hand, I think he would have been congratulated for trapping me, and I would have gotten the criticism.

As a side note, if James had raised me out of the pot, Chip Reese would have made a pair of Kings and remained in the tournament with approximately 600,000 in chips.

When all is said and done,
if I spent most of
my time sitting
at a poker table,
I would feel that
I was a loser
in the game of life.

PARTING
THOUGHTS

Your goal in
life should not be
to make money,
but making money may
help you achieve
your goals.

Where you spend your
time is not nearly
as important as
what you do when
you are there.

PART IV

ADDENDA

Tables for Hold'em after the Flop

IF THE NUMBER OF OUTS IS KNOWN, WHAT IS THE CHANCE OF WINNING?

After the flop, one hand is now the best hand and the other hands are drawing to beat it. It is instructive to know the odds of a drawing hand beating the hand in the lead. However, this knowledge is far less important than using your poker ability to figure out your opponent's hand and how to play accordingly.

In a heads-up pot, if you know your hand, your opponent's hand, and the flop, how many possible combinations are there for the turn and the river? Since you see seven cards, there are 45 possible cards for the turn and 44 possible river cards. Therefore, there are 45 x 44 = 1980 possible combinations. But we are counting every combination twice, since the turn-river combination 7♥ J♠ is the same as the turn-river combination J♠ 7♥. So we divide by 2 and find there are 990 different turn-river combinations when we know two hands and the flop.

When we talk about "outs" we mean the number of cards the current losing hand can hit to become the winning hand. For example, gut-shots have 4 outs, open-end straight draws have 8 outs, and flush draws have 9 outs if the opponent doesn't have one of the needed cards.

Tables for Hold'em after the Flop

TYPICAL DRAWING HANDS THAT PRODUCE A CERTAIN NUMBER OF OUTS ON THE FLOP IN HOLD'EM

Outs	Hand Types
1	lower set; gut-shot straight-flush draw
2	under pair needing trips; open-ended straight-flush draw
3	one overcard vs. a pair; worse kicker, other card the same, whether it pairs the board or not
4	gut-shot; two pair needing to fill up to win
5	pair and a side card
6	two unpaired cards, where pairing either will win
7	set on flop against straight or flush; straight draw with one card unavailable*; flush draw with two cards unavailable*
8	straight draw; flush draw with one card unavailable*
9	flush draw; pair and a gut-shot
10	pair and a straight draw, needing trips or better
11	pair and a flush draw, needing trips or better
12	gut-shot and a flush draw
13	pair and a straight draw; pair and a flush draw with one card unavailable*
14	pair and a flush draw; straight draw with two overcards
15	straight and a flush draw; flush draw with two overcards
16	same as 17, with one card unavailable*
17	straight and a flush draw and a pair, needing trips or better
18	straight and a flush draw and an overcard; gut-shot and a flush draw and two overcards
19	same as 20, with one card unavailable*
20	straight and a flush draw and a pair needing two pair
21	straight and a flush draw and two overcards

Ace on the River

Outs	Hand Types
22	*not possible on the flop in hold'em*
23	straight and a flush draw and board paired against an underpair
24+	*cannot have 24 or more outs on the flop in hold'em* However, with one card to come, there are examples with 25 wins out of 44 cards when the board is paired and one hand has a straight and flush draw with overcards against an underpair.

Also, we can construct an example with 19 wins and 25 ties out of 44 cards with one to come, so that the current winning hand can never win.

Example: 7♣ 2♥ vs. 5♠ 4♠, board shows 6♣ 6♠ 3♥ 3♠.

*A card is unavailable if it is in the opponent's hand or if it improves the opponent's hand to a better one than the drawing hand will make.

To find the probability of hitting your outs when you have two chances, the turn and the river, it is not correct to double the probability of hitting with one card coming. Why? Doubling doesn't work because it is slightly easier to hit on the river, once the draw is missed on the turn. Also, doubling would be the right approach if double credit were given when the outs are hit on both the turn and the river.

For example, suppose we have 9 outs. We have a probability of 9/45 of hitting on the turn. The other 36/45 of the time that we missed, we have a 9/44 chance of hitting on the river. Therefore, we don't add 9/45 more, but instead we add (36/45) x (9/44), which is less. So the chance of hitting a 9-outer on either the turn or the river is

$$\text{Probability of 9-outer} = 9/45 + (36/45) \times (9/44)$$
$$= 198/990 + 162/990$$

(using 990 as a common denominator since we know there are 990 possibilities)

$$= 360/990$$

Tables for Hold'em after the Flop

So there are 360 ways to hit, and 660 ways to miss. If you have done these kinds of calculations before, you probably know that it is simpler to figure out the probability of missing the draw twice and using that number to find out the probability of the draw-out.

If we count the outs of the current losing hand, we can use a similar calculation to determine how many of the 990 combinations will produce a draw-out. Of course, sometimes there are two-card ("runner-runner") outs and sometimes the current winning hand will redraw and win. Also, the current winning hand may hit a card that reduces the number of outs that the drawing hand can hit on the river. To make a first estimate, let's assume that if the drawing hand hits one of its outs, it wins, and let's not count runner-runner outs. The following table gives the results.

Ace on the River

Outs	Wins	Losses	Percent	Odds Against	Odds For
1	44	946	4.44%	21.50 to 1	
2	87	903	8.79%	10.38 to 1	
3	129	861	13.03%	6.67 to 1	
4	170	820	17.17%	4.82 to 1	
5	210	780	21.21%	3.71 to 1	
6	249	741	25.15%	2.98 to 1	
7	287	703	28.99%	2.45 to 1	
8	324	666	32.73%	2.06 to 1	
9	360	630	36.36%	1.75 to 1	
10	395	595	39.90%	1.51 to 1	
11	429	561	43.33%	1.31 to 1	
12	462	528	46.67%	1.14 to 1	
13	494	496	49.90%	1.00 to 1	1.00 to 1
14	525	465	53.03%		1.13 to 1
15	555	435	56.06%		1.28 to 1
16	584	406	58.99%		1.44 to 1
17	612	378	61.82%		1.62 to 1
18	639	351	64.55%		1.82 to 1
19	665	325	67.17%		2.05 to 1
20	690	300	69.70%		2.30 to 1
21	714	276	72.12%		2.59 to 1
22	*It is not possible to have 22 outs on the flop in hold'em.*				
23	759	231	76.67%		3.29 to 1

Tables for Hold'em after the Flop

THE MOST COMMON USE OF THE TABLE

When you have a straight draw with 8 outs, you are slightly worse than a 2 to 1 underdog. You also have 8 outs when you have a flush draw and your opponent has one of your suit. When you have a flush draw with an overcard, you will have 11 or 12 outs and you will be a slight underdog. When you have a flush draw with a pair, you will have 13 or 14 outs and are around even money if your opponent has a card in your suit and a slight favorite if he doesn't.

NOTE ABOUT DIRECT OUTS THAT RESULT IN A TIE

The table doesn't account for confrontations with outs that result in a tie. For example, the case of Q♥ J♥ vs. Q♠ 2♠ with a flop of 10♦ 9♣ 8♣ could be considered one and a half outs since the drawing hand can catch any of three Jacks for a tie.

The following table gives some specific examples in which two-card outs and redraws come into play. If you study examples where the direct number of outs is the same, you will get a better feel for the strength of your hands on the flop.

For each number of direct outs, this table includes a worst-case scenario, a typical scenario, and a best-case scenario for the hand that is behind on the flop.

Outs	Hands	Flop	Wins	Losses	Percent	Against Draw	Odds For Draw
0	A♠ K♠ vs. Q♠ J♠	J♥ J♦ J♣	0	990	0%	---	
0	A♥ A♣ vs. Q♠ J♠	10♠ 9♥ 8♣	32.5	957.5	3.28%	29.46 to 1	
0	A♣ J♥ vs. 10♠ 9♣	10♥ 9♥ 2♣	122	868	12.32%	7.11 to 1	
1	K♠ K♥ vs. A♠ K♣	A♠ 6♦ 2♦	33	957	3.33%	29.00 to 1	
1	6♥ 5♥ vs. A♥ 2♥	9♥ 8♥ 3♥	44	946	4.44%	21.50 to 1	
1	3♣ 3♥ vs. 4♣ 3♦	5♥ 5♣ 4♥	137	853	13.84%	6.23 to 1	
2	9♣ 5♣ vs. J♣ J♥	K♥ Q♥ 10♥	46	944	4.65%	20.52 to 1	
2	9♥ 5♥ vs. A♥ 2♥	J♥ 10♥ 8♥	86	904	8.69%	10.51 to 1	
2	5♣ 2♠ vs. 6♥ 3♥	7♥ 4♣ 4♥	273.5	716.5	27.63%	2.62 to 1	
3	K♠ 8♥ vs. K♥ Q♥	J♥ 10♥ K♣	75	915	7.58%	12.20 to 1	
3	10♥ 9♣ vs. A♣ 9♥	9♦ 7♣ 3♣	158	832	15.96%	5.27 to 1	
3	5♣ 2♥ vs. 6♣ 3♣	7♥ 4♦ 4♣	430.5	559.5	43.48%	1.30 to 1	

Tables for Hold'em after the Flop

Outs	Hands	Flop	Wins	Losses	Percent	Against Draw	Odds For Draw
4	8♣7♣ vs. K♥Q♥	J♣10♥2♥	86	914	8.69%	10.51 to 1	
4	K♣J♠ vs. Q♦10♣	K♥J♠9♦	177.5	812.5	17.93%	4.58 to 1	
4	5♣4♣ vs. 6♥3♥	7♥2♣2♥	343.5	646.5	34.70%	1.88 to 1	
5	8♣7♥ vs. K♣Q♣	J♣10♣10♣	103.5	886.5	10.45%	8.57 to 1	
5	9♥7♣ vs. K♣J♣	J♥7♣2♦	198	792	20.00%	4.00 to 1	
5	4♣3♥ vs. 5♣2♥	10♣9♣6♣	347	643	35.05%	1.85 to 1	
6	8♣7♥ vs. K♣Q♣	J♣10♣10♣	121.5	868.5	12.27%	7.15 to 1	
6	Q♣J♥ vs. 4♣3♣	A♣7♣3♦	244	746	24.65%	3.06 to 1	
6	5♣4♣ vs. 6♥3♥	7♣2♣2♣	547	443	55.25%		1.23 to 1
7	9♣7♥ vs. A♥Q♥	J♣10♥2♥	173	817	17.47%	4.72 to 1	
7	K♥K♣ vs. 8♣7♣	Q♣6♣3♣	312	678	31.52%	2.17 to 1	
7	5♣4♣ vs. 6♥2♥	7♥3♣3♥	411.5	578.5	41.57%	1.41 to 1	

Outs	Hands	Flop	Wins	Losses	Percent	Against Draw	Odds For Draw
8	9♠7♥ vs. A♠Q♠	J♠10♣10♣	191.5	798.5	19.34%	4.17 to 1	
8	9♥8♠ vs. A♠A♣	7♠6♠2♣	327	663	33.03%	2.03 to 1	
8	4♠3♠ vs. 5♥2♠	10♥7♥6♥	431	559	43.54%	1.30 to 1	
9	9♠8♠ vs. A♠10♠	Q♠J♠J♣	220.5	769.5	22.27%	3.49 to 1	
9	10♥9♥ vs. K♦K♣	A♥6♥2♠	371	619	37.47%	1.67 to 1	
9	5♠4♠ vs. 6♠2♥	7♠3♠3♣	639	351	64.55%		1.82 to 1
10	9♠8♠ vs. A♥Q♥	J♥10♥10♣	250.5	739.5	25.30%	2.95 to 1	
10	7♠7♥ vs. 8♠6♠	8♥6♠5♣	351	639	35.45%	1.82 to 1	
10	5♠4♠ vs. 7♥6♥	A♠2♠2♣	587.5	402.5	59.34%		1.46 to 1
11	9♠8♥ vs. A♠Q♠	J♠10♠10♣	272.5	717.5	27.53%	2.63 to 1	
11	9♥7♥ vs. Q♠4♥	Q♥7♠4♥	392	598	39.60%	1.53 to 1	
11	4♠2♥ vs. 5♥3♥	10♠7♠6♠	590.5	399.5	59.65%		1.48 to 1

Tables for Hold'em after the Flop

Outs	Hands	Flop	Wins	Losses	Percent	Against Draw	Odds For Draw
12	9♠8♠ vs. A♣Q♠	J♠10♣2♠	316	674	31.92%	2.13 to 1	
12	10♥8♥ vs. K♠J♦	K♥7♥6♣	478	512	48.28%	1.07 to 1	
12	4♣2♣ vs. 5♥3♥	10♣7♣6♠	613.5	376.5	61.97%		1.63 to 1
13	9♣8♣ vs. A♣Q♠	J♠J♣10♣	335.5	654.5	33.89%	1.95 to 1	
13	7♣6♣ vs. K♥K♣	8♣6♦5♣	475	515	47.98%	1.08 to 1	
13	4♣3♥ vs. 5♥2♣	10♣9♣6♠	655	335	66.16%		1.96 to 1
14	9♣7♣ vs. 10♠10♥	Q♠J♠10♣	355.5	634.5	35.91%	1.78 to 1	
14	A♥6♥ vs. J♠10♣	10♥6♠3♥	511	479	51.62%		1.07 to 1
14	4♣3♥ vs. 5♥2♥	10♠9♣7♠	686	304	69.29%		2.26 to 1
15	9♣2♥ vs. Q♣Q♥	Q♥J♥10♥	389.5	600.5	39.34%	1.54 to 1	
15	9♣8♣ vs. A♣J♦	J♣10♥3♣	553	437	55.86%		1.27 to 1
15	4♠3♥ vs. 5♥2♥	10♣9♣7♠	711.5	278.5	71.87%		2.55 to 1

Outs	Hands	Flop	Wins	Losses	Percent	Against Draw	Odds For Draw
16	9♠8♠ vs. A♣10♥	Q♠J♠J♣	492.5	497.5	49.75%	1.01 to 1	
16	7♥6♦ vs. 10♠9♠	9♦8♦7♠	541	449	54.65%		1.20 to 1
16	4♠3♥ vs. 5♥2♥	10♠7♠6♠	734.5	255.5	74.19%		2.87 to 1
17	K♠K♥ vs. Q♠Q♥	Q♥J♥10♥	486	504	49.09%	1.04 to 1	
17	7♦6♦ vs. 9♠8♣	9♦8♦7♣	541.5	448.5	54.70%		1.21 to 1
17	5♠4♠ vs. 6♥2♥	7♠3♠3♣	762.5	227.5	77.02%		3.35 to 1
18	9♠7♠ vs. A♥Q♥	J♠10♠10♣	539.5	450.5	54.49%		1.20 to 1
18	Q♣9♣ vs. J♥7♥	J♣10♠10♠	583	407	58.89%		1.43 to 1
18	5♠4♠ vs. 7♥6♥	A♠2♠2♣	733.5	256.5	74.09%		2.86 to 1
19	9♣8♣ vs. A♠Q♥	J♣10♠10♣	570.5	419.5	57.63%		1.36 to 1
19	10♠9♠ vs. A♠J♥	8♠7♦3♠	613	377	61.92%		1.63 to 1
19	5♠4♠ vs. 6♥2♠	A♣7♠3♠	692	298	69.90%		2.32 to 1

Outs	Hands	Flop	Wins	Losses	Percent	Against Draw	Odds For Draw
20	5♣4♣ vs. 5♥3♥	6♠6♥3♣	582.5	407.5	58.84%		1.43 to 1
20	10♥7♥ vs. A♣J♠	9♥8♥3♣	660	330	66.67%		2.00 to 1
20	7♣6♣ vs. 8♥2♥	5♣4♣4♣	703.5	286.5	71.06%		2.46 to 1
21	Q♣J♣ vs. A♥10♥	10♥9♣9♥	606	384	61.21%		1.58 to 1
21	J♦10♦ vs. 8♥6♠	9♥9♣8♦	657	333	66.30%		1.97 to 1
21*	K♦Q♦ vs. 2♣2♥	J♦10♦3♣	716	274	72.32%		2.61 to 1
21	7♣6♣ vs. 9♥2♥	5♣4♣4♣	721	269	72.83%		2.68 to 1
23	5♣4♣ vs. 2♣2♥	7♣6♣6♣	666.5	323.5	67.32%		2.06 to 1
23	J♦10♦ vs. 5♥5♥	9♥8♦8♣	689.5	300.5	69.35%		2.29 to 1
23*	K♦Q♦ vs. 2♣2♥	J♦10♦10♣	707.5	282.5	71.46%		2.50 to 1

Ace on the River

Noteworthy information from the table

1. Some hands with 6 outs are favorites and some hands with 17 outs are underdogs.

2. When you are drawing and your opponent flops a set, you would gain a lot of equity if you made an "insurance deal" based on the direct outs, as is commonly done.

3. There are hands with 2 outs that are in better shape than hands with 11 outs.

4. There are match-ups where both hands are the same, yet a flop with fewer direct outs yields a better chance of winning. See the two entries marked with *.

5. There are match-ups with the same number of outs where the drawing hand in one match-up is in twice as good shape as the drawing hand in another match-up. This is not surprising to stud players who are used to making decisions based on their two-card outs and redraw possibilities on fourth and fifth street.

The odds stated are correct only if there is no other information. Once a third player is in the pot, the odds will change somewhat. If the third person folds quickly for a bet on the flop, he is unlikely to have cards that pair the board or make up a straight or a flush draw. If you get to see the third person's cards, it may change the number of outs and will reduce the number of unknown cards to 43. If the third hand didn't contain any of the drawing hand's outs, the drawing hand will have a better chance of winning than has been stated in the tables. Take the example where there are 43 unknown cards and 8 outs for the drawing hand. Not considering two-card outs and redraws, the drawing hand is a 1.93 to 1 underdog, instead of the 2.06 to 1 underdog it would be with 45 unknown cards. You normally don't want to make a side bet with someone who has seen two cards and knows how they relate to the hands in question. In some games, where anyone is allowed to bet on insurance, players out of the hand may quietly discuss what they threw away or may even pick up the muck, which gives them an advantage because they know how the drawing hand's outs are affected.

Tables for Hold'em after the Flop

NOTE ABOUT ODDS DURING THE PLAY OF THE HAND

Most authors use the number 47 for the number of unknown cards during the play of a hand because they don't know their opponent's exact two cards. The odds for the drawing hand are typically better than the result obtained using 47 unknown cards, since there are usually more two-card outs than redraws. For example, if the flop is J♥ 5♣ 2♥ and you have 10♥ 9♥ and you put your opponent on an overpair, you have 9 outs out of 47 cards, which is 1.86 to 1 against making the flush. But if the overpair is Aces, the odds against the drawing hand winning will be 1.73 to 1 on average, taking into consideration cases with and without the Ace of hearts. If the overpair is Queens, which hurts the back-door straights, the odds are 1.80 to 1 against on average. These numbers are closer to the 1.75 to 1 odds in the table of outs given earlier, which uses 45 unknown cards. Another reason to use odds based on 45 unknown cards is the calculation of insurance when both hands are shown. In that case, odds using the number 47 are irrelevant, while odds using the number 45 are useful.

Whether you use 45 or 47 unknown cards, the difference in the odds you obtain will be so small that it is unlikely to affect your play. But using the number 47 suggests a philosophical misunderstanding of poker and how to use mathematics to analyze it. Once your opponent looks at his hole cards and takes action, those cards are no longer unknown. As a matter of fact, once he looks at his cards and you sense anything at all, his cards cannot be considered random.

Bibliography

Bernstein, Carl and Woodward, Bob, 1991, *All the President's Men,* Simon & Schuster

Feller, William, 1968, *An Introduction to Probability Theory and Its Applications, Volume 1, Third Edition,* John Wiley & Sons

Gleick, James, 1987, *Chaos,* Heinemann

Myerson, Roger B., 1991, *Game Theory: Analysis of Conflict,* Harvard University Press

Packel, Edward, 1981, *The Mathematics of Games and Gambling,* The Mathematical Association of America

Peter, Lawrence J. and Hill, Raymond, 1969, *Peter Principle,* William Morrow & Company, Inc.

Roland, Per E., 1993, *Brain Activation,* Wiley-Liss, Inc

Skinner, B. F., 1938, *Schedules of Reinforcement*

Glossary

Ante Money put into the pot by each player before a hand is dealt so that players have something to win.

Bad beat Losing a hand when winning seemed very likely.

Betting lead The player who made the last bet or raise on a betting round is said to have the *betting lead* for the next round of betting during a hand.

Big bet In limit poker, the limit on the final betting round. Example: In a $20-$40 game, a $20 bet on the early round is called the small bet, whereas the $40 bet on the later rounds is called the big bet.

Blinds A method of getting money into the pot before a hand is dealt. Normally, blinds are used as an alternative to antes. In the most common blind structure, the first two players to the left of the dealer put money in the pot and the action starts with the next player folding, calling, or raising the *blind* bet of the player to his right.

Bluff A bet or a raise with the purpose of getting your opponent to fold when you believe he has a better hand than you have.

Burn A card that is dealt down after a betting round and before players get cards for the next betting round. For example, in hold'em a card is burned before the flop, turn, and river. This is done as a precaution so players cannot take action while seeing any part of the next card to be dealt.

Button games Poker games, such as hold'em and draw poker, where the betting goes in order ending up with the dealer acting last. As the dealer position is rotated, a button is moved to indicate whose turn it is to deal. The button is normally a white round piece of plastic about half the size of a hockey puck.

Buy-in The minimum amount required to play in a poker game or tournament.

Cap The maximum number of raises allowed on a betting round in limit poker. In no-limit, it refers to the maximum loss any player is allowed to have on a hand.

Check-raise A tactic of checking when it is one's turn to act when there are opponents behind and then raising after one of those opponents bets. The initial check represents a weak hand and the subsequent raise represents a very strong hand, essentially signifying that the check-raiser checked only to mislead his opponents.

Chinese poker A game in which each player is dealt thirteen cards to be arranged in three hands: a three card hand and two five card hands. The hands are set in ascending order of strength, with the three card hand being the weakest. Players then compare the three hands to those of their opponents, receiving a point for each instance the poker hand at that position is stronger than the corresponding hand of an opponent.

Coffee-housers Players who do a lot of acting to deceive their opponents about the strength of their hand.

Community cards Also called *common cards*. Cards that all players can use, which in some forms of poker are dealt face up after players get their hands.

Dealer The person dealing the cards or, in a button game, the player whose turn it is to have the button and therefore has last action on betting rounds.

Draw out Receiving one or more cards which changes a losing hand to a winning hand.

Draw poker Poker game in which each player receives five cards and, after a betting round, is allowed to replace any number of cards.

Flop The first three community cards in games such as hold'em and Omaha, which have five community cards.

Free card When all players check on a betting street with more cards to come, a player who is a favorite to win is said to have given his opponents a *free card* instead of making them pay when they are at a disadvantage. (Even if he did bet, it may be correct for them to call because of equity they have from money already in the pot.) Occasionally, a player will intentionally give free cards to mislead opponents about the strength of his hand.

Freeroll A situation in which someone can win, but can't lose. For example, in seven-card stud, when two players each have an Ace-high straight with one card to come, but one has a flush draw, the player with the flush draw is on a freeroll.

Good game A game that is lucrative because there are several weak players playing.

High-low poker A form of poker where the highest hand and the lowest hand split the pot. If one player holds both the highest and lowest hands, he *scoops* the whole pot. The most common forms are seven-card stud high-low and Omaha Eight-or-better. When a game is designated as Eight-or-better, players are required to have an Eight-low or better to qualify for the low half of the pot. If no one qualifies, the high hand scoops the pot.

High poker The form of poker in which a player uses his best five cards to make a hand. The best hand is a *royal flush*, which is A K Q J 10 of the same suit, unless wild cards are used, in which case five Aces is the best hand. The most common variants of high poker are hold'em and seven-card stud.

Hold'em Poker game in which each player receives two *hole cards*, and players who call in each betting round can use five community ("board") cards. The community cards are dealt three on the *flop*, one on the *turn*, and one on the *river*. Each player's final hand is the best five-card poker hand made from any of the seven usable cards — his two hole cards and the five board cards.

Hole cards The cards in a player's hand that opponents are not allowed to see, as opposed to the upcards.

Implied odds The odds one is getting, including money that is not yet in the pot, but is expected to go into the pot on subsequent betting rounds.

Insurance A proportionate splitting of the pot before a hand is completed, based on each player's chances of winning.

Laydown Not calling an opponent's bet, thereby forfeiting a chance to win the pot. Also called a *fold*.

Limit poker A betting structure with fixed bet amounts in each betting interval. For example, in $20-$40 limit hold'em, all bets and raises are $20 in the first two betting intervals and $40 in the last two betting intervals.

Limp Enter a pot for the minimum amount, which is normally the amount of a forced bet.

Live one A player who loses a lot of money playing poker. Obviously, someone you want in your game.

Lowball A form of poker in which the lowest hand wins. An Ace is the lowest card and the best possible low hand is A 2 3 4 5, which is called a *wheel*. A variant in which Aces are high and straights and flushes are counted adversely is called Deuce-to-Seven lowball, since the best hand is 7 5 4 3 2 with at least one card not the same suit as the others. In lowball, hands are denoted by their highest card. For example, 9 8 5 4 2 is called a Nine-low, even though Nine is actually the highest card in the hand. The most common variants are seven-card stud low, which is called *razz*, and triple-draw lowball.

Make-up figure Cumulative amount that a player being staked has lost. Usually this has to be won back before the player can collect some money when he wins.

Murphy's Law If anything can go wrong, it will.

Nitty Tight with money and very conservative when gambling.

No-limit poker A betting structure in which players are allowed to bet any amount of the chips in front of them. If a bet is made that is larger than the amount a player has, he is only liable for the amount in front of him, and that is also all he can win from another player.

Nuts A hand that can't lose or a situation where there is no possibility of losing.

Omaha A poker game in which each player gets four *hole cards*, and players who call in each betting round can use five common cards. The common cards are dealt in hold'em style: three on the flop, one on the turn, and one on the river. In Omaha, players must use two cards in their hands and three from the common cards. For example, if there are four spades among the common cards, a player with only one spade in his hand does not have a flush as he would in hold'em.

Outs The number of cards remaining in the deck that will enable one hand to beat another.

Pat hand In draw poker, when a player keeps the cards originally dealt to him and doesn't draw any cards. Also, hands that have the ranking of a straight or better are sometimes called *pat hands*.

Peter Principle In a hierarchy, employees tend to be promoted to the level of their incompetence.

Poker games The most common forms of poker played today are hold'em, seven-card stud, five-card draw, Omaha, triple-draw lowball, and variations where the highest hand and the lowest hand split the pot.

Position Betting order in a poker game. 1) *Entry position* refers to the first round of betting. For example, in games with a button, early entry position usually refers to the first few positions after the big blind. In games where the high or low card acts first, the next few players are in early position. 2) *Betting position* refers to subsequent rounds of betting. In games with a dealer button, the player to the left of the button is in first position. In games where players have upcards, the player with the highest hand (lowest hand for low games) is in first position. 3) *Having position on a player* means being able to act (check, bet, call, or raise) after that player has acted. Usually, you have position on a player because you are sitting to his left or because his upcards are higher than yours.

Pot limit A betting structure in which players can bet up to the current amount of the pot. For example, if there is $100 in the pot, the first player to act may bet $100 and the next player is allowed to call the $100 and raise up to $300 more.

Rake Table fees. (*See time.*)

Rebuy The act of buying more chips to play, normally because one has no chips or very few chips. Some tournament events allow participants to rebuy during the first few levels as a way of increasing the prize pool.

Ring game A full game, usually eight, nine, or ten handed, as opposed to a short-handed game.

River The last betting interval in a poker hand. Also, the last community card in a game that uses them.

Satellite A small tournament, usually one table, where the winner is awarded an entry into a larger buy-in tournament.

Scoop Winning the whole pot in split-pot games such as seven-card stud high-low.

Scrambling Putting the cards in a scattered pile on the table and moving them around to mix up their order.

Semi-bluff A bet or raise with a hand that has several outs against likely hands your opponent may have, so you win if he folds or if you draw out.

Seven-card stud Poker game in which each player gets two cards down and one card up. The betting starts with the player who has the lowest upcard. Players who have called all bets on each round get three more upcards and the seventh card down.

Showdown A form of poker that eliminates the skill factor, in which all betting is done before the hands are dealt. Also, the *showdown* is the event at the end of a poker hand during which each remaining player shows his hand.

Side games Poker games going on during a tournament that are not part of the tournament. Also called *live action or cash games*.

Slowroll Teasing the opponent by not showing the winning hand until the opponent thinks he has won.

Stake To put up money for someone else to play for a percentage of the winnings.

Stakehorse A player put in a game, or staked, by another person.

Steam point The amount a player has to lose before his playing ability drastically deteriorates.

Street An interval in a poker hand where betting is allowed. There are two streets in lowball, four streets in hold'em, and five streets in seven-card stud. The last three streets in hold'em are called the flop, the turn, and the river.

String raise Making a raise by putting money in the pot and then, in a separate motion, getting additional chips from one's stack to increase the bet.

Supersatellite A multiple table tournament, usually allowing rebuys, where the top few finishers are each awarded entries into a larger buy-in tournament.

Swap pieces Two players of comparable skill may take a small percentage of each other's action. Tournament players do this to even out the luck and increase their enjoyment.

Sweaters People who watch a card game. Also called *kibitzers*.

Tell A player's mannerism that gives away the strength of his hand.

Tilt More commonly *on tilt*. To play very badly because of previous losses or other upsetting circumstances.

Time The table fees an establishment charges — usually around $30 an hour per player in high-stakes games. Also called the *rake*, the *drop*, or the *take*.

Top pair In a game with common cards such as hold'em, a pair made by a player holding a *hole card* of the same rank as the highest common card. If one of his *hole cards* pairs the second highest common card, the player has *second pair*. If it pairs the lowest common card, he has *bottom pair*.

Triple-draw A type of draw poker in which players are allowed to draw three times with betting after each draw. This is usually played as a form of lowball.

Turn A player's turn to fold, bet, check, or raise. Also, the fourth community card in games such as hold'em and Omaha that have five community cards.

Value-bet A bet made by a player with a mediocre hand when he thinks his hand is slightly better than his opponents' hands. A *value-bet* is occasionally made by a player in early betting position even when he thinks he probably doesn't have the best hand, but he is catering to the possibility that his opponents will check on the occasions when he has them beat.

Victory rip The triumphant showing of a probable winning hand.

Vigorish The commission paid on a sports bet in return for the right to chose which side to bet on.

Walk Winning of a pot by a player whose bet, usually a forced bet, is not called in the first betting round.

Weighted Giving different value to different factors.

Went in the tank Took a long time to make a decision.

Wrap A straight draw in Omaha where more than two different card ranks will fill the straight.

Index

List of Photographs
(by Page)

Acknowledgements

In order of time spent helping me:

Jack Greenstein – my father and chief editor. He spent several months carefully changing words and rewriting paragraphs. This resulted in many hours on the phone going over his suggestions. His drive and attention to detail would be amazing, even if he wasn't ninety years old.

Charles Kaine – the publisher and the director of the project. Charles organized the book and oversaw the publication.

Joan Winn – my sister. She helped me focus the perspective of the manuscript and offered editing advice. She also reorganized the *Gambling and Productive Society* chapter.

Molly Ball – my niece. I dictated some poker stories to her that evolved into the *My Poker Career* chapter. Molly also did extensive editing.

Eric Drache – poker player and card room manager extraordinaire. Eric provided me with stories of old Las Vegas and critiqued the early versions of the manuscript.

Steve Brecher – tournament player. He offered editorial help in return for reading an early copy of the manuscript. Steve made many critical corrections.

Alexandra Vuong – my partner. Alex typed from my handwritten notes at the start of the project and tolerated the hours I spent neglecting her while completing it.

Sandie Linn – my younger sister. I discussed many ideas with her, and she also was the arbitrator when my father and I disagreed.

Sharon Fletcher – my first girlfriend whom I haven't seen in over thirty years. She contributed about a hundred corrections. I want to also thank her husband Dan for supporting the collaboration.

Joseph Sebok – my son. He took up poker during the writing of this book which provided me with his perspective as an inexperienced player. Joe also found several errors in the no-limit tournament hand diagrams.

Phil Ivey – great player and friend. Phil gave me several ideas that I used in the *Poker on the Internet* chapter.

Avery Cardoza – highest-selling poker book publisher. Avery came up with the idea of prefacing each chapter with an explanation.

David Heyden – friend, top player, and student of the game. David read early versions of the manuscript and offered suggestions.

Peter Ampudia – psychiatrist specializing in family therapy. Peter helped me with the *Poker and Your Family* chapter and validated some of my homespun psychology.

Howard Greenstein – my brother. He read the first draft of the manuscript and gave me emotional support as he always does.

Michael Sebok – my son. Michael came on board late, but helped by proofreading the final versions.

Mori Eskandani – winning player and technical advisor for many televised poker shows. Mori verified the no-limit tournament hand diagrams.

Jim Tarr – friend, engineer, and poker player. Jim gave me a list of points that needed clarification.

Brian Saliba – wrote the first critical review. This helped me make smoother transitions and make the text more relevant.

Phil Laak – well-known tournament player. I included an explanation of the win-rate calculations as a result of his comments.

Chad Brown – top player and poker announcer. With Chad's help, I clarified the explanation of the odds for Ace-King versus small pairs in hold'em.

GRAPHICS DESIGN TEAM

Gregg Kantz – sculptor. He was in charge of graphic design for *Ace on the River*. Gregg turned the manuscript into a work of art. Many people will enjoy his photographs more than the written content.

Brad Dunbar – designer. Brad assisted in all aspects of the book's creation. From text formatting, honest critique, type changes, to photography and design, he was an invaluable resource.

Elissa Quist – graphic artist. Elissa's keen eye for detail was essential, especially with regard to the front cover.

Julie Lovell – graphic artist. Julie is a top-notch graphics professional who helped primarily with the chapter headings.

Michael St. Clair – design reviewer. Michael proofread the final versions from a graphical perspective and found justification mistakes and some other errors.

Gregg would like to thank the casino personnel who allowed him to photograph their facilities. Some shots were taken in sensitive areas of the casino, and more than a few eyebrows were raised while he was lying on his back taking pictures of the ceiling, or when he was carrying his 70-pound camera into the poker room. Additional thanks go to Shane Henman of Maverick Poker Tables for providing material to construct artificial poker tables.